William Lucas Sargant

Apology for Sinking-Funds

William Lucas Sargant
Apology for Sinking-Funds
ISBN/EAN: 9783743407220
Manufactured in Europe, USA, Canada, Australia, Japa
Cover: Foto ©Thomas Meinert / pixelio.de

Manufactured and distributed by brebook publishing software (www.brebook.com)

William Lucas Sargant

Apology for Sinking-Funds

FOR

SINKING-FUNDS:

BY

WILLIAM LUCAS SARGANT,

AUTHOR OF "SOCIAL INNOVATORS," &c.

LONDON:
WILLIAMS AND NORGATE, HENRIETTA ST., COVENT GARDEN,
AND
SOUTH FREDERICK STREET, EDINBURGH.

1868.

BIRMINGHAM:
PRINTED BY MARTIN BILLING, SON, AND CO.,
LIVERY STREET.

PREFACE.

IN the last generation, the National Debt was a bugbear which oppressed the spirits of Englishmen. Taxation was burdensome to a degree hardly conceivable by the young men of to-day: and of the scores of millions annually raised, more than half went to pay interest due to the public creditors.

Elderly men remember the time when the subject was discussed at the fireside of everyone who read a newspaper: when Attwood's "little shilling" and Cobbett's "sponge," divided the allegiance of the middle classes.

Gradually, the nation became inured to the load: as prosperity returned, as population multiplied, as opulence grew, the weight was less felt.

Besides; though the principal of the debt remained nearly stationary, the rate of interest was much reduced; and frugality was forced on the government by the public. During the twenty years between 1831 and 1850* the taxes were only about 2£ a head of population; less by a fifth than they had been between 1821 and 1830, and about half what they had been towards the close of the war.

Increasing opulence and decreasing taxation brought a sense of relief. The minds of men too,

---

* L. Levi, Taxation 25.

were diverted to political questions: to the repeal of the Test Acts; to the emancipation of the Roman Catholics; to the severe and long struggle which carried the Reform Bill; to the extinction of slavery; to the repeal of the Corn Laws; to the reconstruction of our fiscal system. The National Debt was forgotten.

It is high time however, that our memory should awake from its slumber: that we should remember how large a portion of our public revenue goes to pay the national creditors: and that we should inquire what is our present duty as to the debt.

The Reform Bill of 1867, has shifted the centre of gravity of the constituent body: although perhaps, the House of Commons may appear little changed, the Members will find an alteration in the influence exercised by their electors. I look without alarm, I look even with much hope, at this great change: I anticipate a renewed energy and a spirit of enterprise, in the conduct of our government. But I feel that those who have incurred our vast debt, and those who have allowed it to remain undiminished during the last thirty years, must be prepared to answer the question which may be put to them in a voice of thunder, whether that debt is to go down unliquidated to our children's children.

The new constituents will doubtless be appealed to by writers and speakers on this grave subject; by new Cobbetts and new Attwoods: it requires no familiarity with Latin verses or with the Calculus, to understand that eight hundred millions were borrowed by our progenitors, that we and our fathers have been paying interest ever since, and that unless some new efforts are made, our posterity will go on paying interest for centuries to come. Plain men will learn with indignation, that even the moderate sinking-fund which was in existence ten years ago in the form of terminable annuities, has been seriously diminished: that it has been reduced from three millions to a million and a half.*

That politician too, must be a fool, or worse than a fool, who would flatter us with dreams of unbroken peace. England, no doubt, has ceased to be the knight-errant of Europe, rushing into every quarrel, claiming to arbitrate in every dispute, interfering in every variation of the shifting balance of power, pretending to protect or avenge every oppressed nationality. Strong but self-restrained, we are too moderate and too formidable to run much danger of being insulted. Yet sooner or later war will come, by the madness of other nations or by unusual follies of our foreign office: war which will cost us, not a few millions like our Abyssinian expedition, but scores or hundreds of millions.

Even in time of peace disasters may overtake us; disasters more formidable than the depression of commerce which follows our decennial inflation and madness. Our coal may fail us: the competition of other nations may rob us of foreign markets; or may so far lower the prices of manufactures as to greatly reduce our rates of wages and profit: our artisans may prefer emigration to poverty; and our population, instead of increasing as heretofore, may become stationary, or may diminish like that of Ireland.

The English would still be a great nation: great in historical freedom, great in agricultural resources, great above all in stubborn force of character. But their greatness would give them no immunity from the pressure of taxation. We can now raise our seventy millions without any intolerable sacrifice: hereafter the same burden may seem too much to be borne.

Ought we not therefore, to inquire seriously what it would cost us to reduce our debt: what, to extinguish it in a hundred years?

In this volume, I have put together facts and reasonings which, I hope, may aid the inquiry. I have come to the conclusion that at a small cost we might establish such a fund, as by mere natural growth would relieve our posterity from all the present debt: that it might be raised in such a way as to interfere in no wise with readjustment of taxation, and not at all to hinder the due accumulation of capital: that it would be free from the insuperable objections which attach to terminable aunuities: that it would be taken out of the jurisdiction of the Chancellor of the Exchequer, and would therefore escape the danger of manipulation and reduction in the annual budget: that it would be intelligible to the whole nation, and would consequently exist under the soundest of all securities, the guarantee of public opinion.

CONTENTS OF CHAPTERS.

CHAPTER	PAGES
I.—First Principles	1 to 27
II.—History of British Sinking-Funds .	28 to 82
III.—Illustration and Explanations . .	83 to 114
IV.—Progress of Debt and Repayment: British and Foreign . . .	115 to 147
V.—Our Present Duty	148 to 220
VI.—How we shall best Perform our Duty	221 to 247

CHAPTER I.

FIRST PRINCIPLES.

I.

THE term Sinking-Fund is familiar to us all; but it may be useful to recall its exact meaning.

Illustration: landed estate: debt on it. I will suppose that I am fortunate enough to succeed to an estate yielding £10,000 a year; burdened however, with a debt of £60,000. I propose to pay off this debt.

For simplicity I will call the rate of interest 5 per cent., and my annual payment for interest therefore, £3,000.

Annual discharge of £1,000. In order to lessen the debt, I may take the obvious course of paying off £1,000 of the principal each year: if I am so singularly fortunate as to enjoy the estate sixty years, I shall discharge the whole debt. By this means the drain on me for interest will diminish each year: for at the end of the first year I shall pay off £1,000 of the principal; and therefore, in the second year my debt will be only £59,000, and my interest £2,950 instead of £3,000; in the third year my interest will be £2,900; in the seventh year £2,500; in the twenty-first year £2,000; in the forty-first year £1,000; in the sixtieth year £50.

The same with compound interest: years 1st to 14th. This annual payment of £1,000, if formally established, constitutes a Sinking-Fund. But I may go a step further. In the former case, my payments were:

B

In the 1st year for interest, £3,000; for principal repaid £1,000 = £4,000.
„ 2nd year „ 2,950; „ 1,000 = 3,950.
„ 3rd year „ 2,900; „ 1,000 = 3,900.

I may determine however, to continue to pay £4,000 every year until the debt of £60,000 is paid off. The £4,000 will be appropriated as follows :—

	For Interest.	Repaid Principal.	Total.	Debt Owing.
1st year ...	£3,000	£1,000	£4,000	£59,000
2nd year	2,950	1,050	4,000	57,950
3rd year	2,897 10 0	1,102 10 0	4,000	56,847 10 0

Under this second arrangement, the principal repaid, instead of being uniformly £1,000, will be in successive years £1,000, £1,050, £1,102 10s., &c.; that is £1,000 increasing at compound interest at the assumed 5 per cent. We all know that in about fourteen years, £100 at 5˙per cent. compound interest becomes £200 : that whereas the simple interest in fourteen years is £70, the compound interest is £100 : it follows that the compound interest which appears in my second table, £1,000, £1,050, £1,102 10s., &c., will in about fourteen years amount to £20,000. While the simple interest would be £14,000, the compound interest would be £6,000 more. This £6,000 is not produced by any trick of figures, but by my continuing to pay a uniform £4,000 a year instead of the constantly diminishing sums £4,000, £3,950, £3,900, &c.

Years 15th to 28th. I begin the fifteenth year then, with a debt reduced from £60,000 to £40,000. I will continue to set aside £4,000 a year; of which in the fifteenth year £2,000 will go to interest and £2,000 to pay off principal. Again, as in the former period, the interest will diminish each year; and the repayment of principal will increase : and as we found that in the former period of 14 years, the series of payments £1,000, £1,050, £1,102 10s., &c., amounted to a total of £20,000, we must conclude that the present series commencing with £2,000 will be double the former one, *i.e.*, will amount to a total in the second 14 years, of £40,000, which will finally discharge the debt.

Comparison, results, simple and compound. It seems then, that whereas by the annual payment of £1,000 during 28 years, I should discharge only £28,000 of debt; by the annual payment of £1,000 plus the compound interest on that sum, I should in the same 28 years discharge the whole £60,000 of debt: the extinction with compound interest would be more than double what it would be with simple interest.

Here again, I must repeat that this is not the result of any trick of figures: that it is the result of my self-denial in continuing to pay annually a total of £4,000 instead of paying constantly diminishing sums, £4,000, £3,950, £3,900, &c.

I might put £20,000 into a trust. The same result might be obtained in another way. Say that on my succeeding to the estate, I at once put into the hands of a trustee a farm worth £20,000, and yielding £1,000 a year; and that he undertakes to invest this £1,000 a year at 5 per cent. compound interest. We know that in about fourteen years, the £20,000 will have become £40,000; and that in 28 years it will have become £80,000. At the end of the 28 years, therefore, the trustee can pay off the £60,000 debt, and restore me my £20,000. As in the former cases, I pay the £3,000 a year interest during the twenty-eight years: *i.e.*, I diminish my income during that period by £4,000 a year; viz., £3,000 which I pay for interest, and £1,000 the rent of the farm in trust.

I might borrow £20,000 and put into a trust. Could I do the same thing by borrowing money? I certainly could. I mean by this that I might borrow at first to form a fund : I do not mean that by borrowing alone I could do anything. Borrow or not, the discharge of the debt can only be effected by the self-denial necessary to save.

Instead of putting into the hands of a trustee, a farm worth £20,000, and yielding £1,000 a year, I may borrow £20,000 and put that sum into the hands of the trustee; in about 28 years the £20,000 will multiply into £80,000; and the trustee can then pay off both the original £60,000, and the subsequent £20,000. But during the 28 years I shall have had to pay the same £4,000 a year, as in the former cases; viz., the interest of £60,000 and of £20,000. I gain nothing by my borrowing the £20,000 : I have even the disadvantage of all the expenses and discredit of borrowing.

Borrowing at simple, accumulating at compound interest. It is true that I do what has been called borrowing at simple interest and accumulating at compound interest; but the whole advantage of the arrangement arises from my paying an uniform sum of £4,000 during the 28 years; i e., after the first year, a sum greater than the simple interest on the debts. It is not the borrowing at simple interest which discharges the principal of the debt: it is the paying off each year a part of the principal.

It is convenient to know, that by paying this uniform £4,000 during about 28 years, I shall get rid of the debt of £60,000; this knowledge furnishes a motive for making this annual payment: but no trick of figures will relieve me from paying the whole £60,000 out of my income. We shall see afterwards however, that this is not the whole truth.

II.

Dr. Price's principle: called Utopian. THIS notion of borrowing at simple interest, and accumulating a fund at compound interest, was preached by Dr. Price and accepted by Mr. Pitt and his friends: though it was no new discovery, it was reproduced as a sure mode of relieving the nation from the load of debt by which it was oppressed. At the present day, the expectation of relief by such means is regarded as of no more value than the expectation of the indefinite perfectibility of man, and the consequent cessation hereafter of pain and death. Price's "Reversionary Annuities," and Godwin's "Political Justice," are put side by side on the Utopian shelf.

Tried by private case. I have shown that the reduction of my debt on the estate is effected by no trick of figures, but by saving from my income. But let us see whether this is the whole truth.

Let us say that on succeeding to my estate, I at once set aside for 28 years £4,000 a year; of which £3,000 goes to pay the annual interest, and £1,000 is invested at 5 per cent. compound interest, and therefore amounts at the end of about 14 years to £20,000, and at the end of about 28 years to £60,000. If I had discharged no principal, I should have paid £3,000 annually during the 28 years; and therefore my additional payment has been £1,000 a year during 28 years, or £28,000.

Next let us imagine that during the first fourteen years after I had succeeded to my estate, I spent the whole income; but that at the end of the fourteen years I set aside for the second fourteen years £2,000 a year, besides the £3,000 for interest. By the end of the 28th year I should have given up towards payment of principal, £2,000 a year during 14 years, or £28,000.

On both these suppositions I have made the same sacrifice of income, viz., £28,000 : the only difference being that in the former case I have sacrificed £1,000 in each of the 28 years, and that in the latter case I have sacrificed £2,000 in each of the latter 14 years.

But though the sacrifices are the same the results are different.

I Have Accumulated :	In the 1st. Case :	In the 2nd Case :
At the end of 14 years,	14 years at £1,000 + Compound Interest £20,000.	Nothing.
At the end of 28 years.	28 years at £1,000 Compound Interest + £60,000.	14 years at £2,000 + Compound Interest £40,000.

In the first case I have accumulated £60,000 ; in the second case only £40,000.

This shows how vital an element time is ; it indicates that the date at which the sacrifices are made is of the highest importance ; and if of importance during the life of a man, far more so during the longer life of a nation.

By supposing a larger debt, and carrying on the process some steps further, we shall find striking results.

1st case, extended. I and my successors set aside £1,000 a year for a very long period ; still continuing to pay, out of income, interest on the debt.

At the end of 14 years, we have accumulated	£20,000
,, 28 ,, ,,	60,000
,, 42 ,, ,,	140,000
,, 56 ,, ,,	260,000
The sacrifices we have made amount to £1,000 for 56 years	= 56,000

2nd case, extended. I and my successors go on during 42 years, spending the whole income left after discharging the annual interest on the debt. At the end of the 42nd year we set aside £4,000 a year as a sinking-fund.

<small>At the end of the 56th year we shall have accumulated £80,000
Our sacrifices will have been .... 14 × £4,000 = 56,000</small>

Comparing these two extended cases, the sacrifices in both cases being £56,000, in the former there is an accumulation of £260,000, in the latter only £80,000. So important an element is time

Least possible sacrifice. It appears therefore, that the earlier I begin to save, the less will be the sacrifice required. To reduce the sacrifice to the lowest possible point, I should, on succeeding to the estate, apply the greater part of the income to constitute a fund. Say that during the two first years, out of the two years' income, I set aside £15,000. After the end of the second year, I should only have to pay £3,000, the interest on the debt, just as if I had not constituted any fund. All my sacrifice will have been £15,000. If we imagine that my successors leave this fund to grow, they will find that at the end of 58 years after I first came into possession, the fund amounts to £240,000.

But we found before that £1,000 a year for 56 years amounts to little more, viz., £260,000, and this with the sacrifice of £56,000, or nearly four times as much.

The principle. The principle therefore, is indisputable: begin your fund as early as possible ; and thus take full advantage of the accumulation by compound interest.

Suppose not land, but money. I will now take a different case, as a means of estimating the force of an objection commonly made. Instead of land, let it be £200,000 in personalty that has been bequeathed to me.

in a business Say further, that this consists of capital engaged in a manufacturing business yielding 10 per cent. on the capital employed : the debt of £60,000 being a mortgage on the factory and land.

incapable of extension If the business is incapable of judicious extension, I may wisely appropriate part of the two first years' profits to form a fund, as in the case of the estate; and if my sons and grandsons leave that fund to grow at 5 per cent., they will find, at the end of 58 years, that it amounts to £240,000; all obtained at the trifling sacrifice on my part of the gratifications purchasable with £15,000.

or capable of extension. But what if the business *is* capable of judicious extension ? What if the £15,000, invested in new buildings and machinery and stock, would yield me the same 10 per cent. that I obtain on my other capital ? In that case I should get a far larger money advantage by so investing it, than by forming a sinking fund with it. Even if I got only 6 per cent. by such a business investment, I should lose by applying the £15,000 to a fund at 5 per cent. It might, even then, be more prudent to form the fund; but it would not be more profitable.

Distinction, Capital, and Self-maintenance, Even in the case of the land, if I could use the £15,000 in draining and building, so as to get 5 per cent. upon it, I should gain nothing by forming a fund with it; if my gain upon it would be 6 per cent., I should lose by forming such a fund.

But in all my previous remarks, I have assumed that the fund is formed by saving from personal expenditure, and not by applying sums which would otherwise be used as capital: I have assumed that instead of spending £7,000 a year on housekeeping, and hunters, and travelling, I have spent only £6,000 a year; or that instead of beginning such expenditure immediately on succeeding to the estate, I have deferred the greater part of it for two years.

or saving and spending. The distinction between personal expenditure and saving, is at the root of the question. If I save £1,000 and use that sum productively, I earn an income from it: if I again save that income and use it productively, my income is further increased; and if I only get 5 per cent., my first £1,000 becomes in about 14 years, £2,000: or if I save £1,000 every year, in about 14 years I shall have £20,000. But if in the first year I spend the £1,000 on a well furnished table and men servants and horses, the money is finally gone: there is no accumulation: the expenditure may be a wise one; but it causes no increase of any kind. If I save this £1,000 each year and put it out to 5 per cent. interest, at the end of about 14 years I possess £20,000; if I spend the £1,000 each year, at the end of the 14 years I have nothing but the memory of past pleasures.

Debt cannot be paid without self-denial: but if self-denial be exercised, it matters not whether the result of it goes to form a separate fund, or is laid out as capital at an equal rate of profit.

We shall see, in the same way, that a national sinking-fund ought to be formed by taxation, and by such taxation as will cause a diminished expenditure on the part of the people.

III.

Evils of borrowing.

BUT why should we not borrow? It is conceded that, individually, we ought not to borrow unless we are compelled to do so, or unless we propose to use the loan as a capital. But why should we not individually borrow to supply our current expenditure?

1st.   When we spend only the income we work for, or what our property furnishes, we have a natural limit to our outlay; but "borrowing dulls the edge of husbandry."

2nd.   Even if our habit of expense be not increased, as in the case where a man borrows to buy books or pictures, and fills his shelves or his walls, yet we are left with a debt which we have to repay. We have first enjoyed the pleasure of acquiring, and afterwards we have to deny ourselves other and accustomed pleasures.

3rd, paying repeatedly.

But besides these evils there is a third and a formidable one: that on which Dr. Price insists with great energy. Among the Hebrews of old, a lender could only reclaim from one of his nation the sum he had lent: among the Mahometans also, interest is forbidden. Among Christian nations, the taking of a reasonable interest is just as reputable a practice as the taking a price for a house or for a load of wheat. Not only have I to return the £1,000 I borrowed, but I have further to pay £50 a year for the use of it: so that, at the end of 20 years, if I have allowed the debt to stand so long, I shall have paid £1,000 for interest, and shall still owe the original sum.

Applied to a nation.

Great Britain has paid the interest on its debt with punctuality; but how vast has been the amount! Calling our average payment since 1815, 30 millions £ a year, we shall have paid altogether in 53 years, no less than 1,590 millions £ : nearly twice over what we owed in 1815. Our debt is now 800 millions £ ; and at an average interest of 24 millions £ a year, we shall pay the 800 millions £ in about 24 years, and shall still owe our present debt. This is the frightful evil against which Dr. Price lifted up his voice.

Two principles. We have now arrived therefore, at two principles : 1st, that the fund should be commenced as early as possible, in order to get the advantage of compound interest ; 2ndly, that it should be formed of such savings from expenditure as would not be otherwise used as capital.

Distinction : individual and nation. It should be observed here however, that my reasonings so far have reference principally to a private estate : I propose to show afterwards that the case of a nation is in one respect different; that though we think of the nation as a unit, it really consists of millions of persons, and of various classes ; and that these persons and classes may be differently affected by the modes of national saving.

Wisdom in individual. Few persons would dispute the wisdom of my supposed conduct, on my imaginary succession to a burdened estate. It may seem obvious too, that a nation loaded with debt would act with equal prudence in creating a sinking-fund.

Why not in nation ? How is it then, that little is done, and that little by annuities and other stealthy means ? If in any budget, during peace, the national expenditure were shown to exceed the income, the Chancellor of the Exchequer would have to give place to a successor : even during war the people would rather submit to a large income-tax than resort principally to loans; witness the fourteen and sixteen pence in the pound, of the Crimean War.

Public indifference. We shrink from contracting debt: we decline all formal means of discharging it. Sir G. C. Lewis made an effort; but in vain: Mr. Gladstone has made several efforts; but with little success.

Example, the "Spectator." Last year Mr. Gladstone proposed a scheme, too complex to be understood by many persons, but approved by competent judges and by a hostile successor, by which, at a moderate annual charge, a considerable amount of debt would be extinguished in the present generation. Now there is no more thoughtful journal than the *Spectator*; no journal which a reader may rely upon with more safety. The editor of that paper spoke, I believe, the sentiments of reflective and high-minded men, when he slighted this scheme of Mr. Gladstone's.

Casual remark. We can often judge better of a man's sentiments from what comes out indirectly, than from his reasonings when he is on his guard. It is a casual expression of the *Spectator* on which I rely. The paragraph has reference to furnishing the army with breech-loading rifles : " We are spending fifteen millions a year upon the army, and then the bureaus are agitated because we spend a million, once for all, to make that army efficient. Let *General Peel* take the million, if necessary, which was to have gone to the National Debt, but let him get the work done, done quickly and done well, and the country will support him."

Shows the indifference. I do not dispute the importance of providing the army with efficient weapons: I grant that the cheapest of all warlike proceedings is to keep our forces in such a state of efficiency, as to warn off trespassers from the soil of England: if the cost were, not one million, but twenty, I should not grudge it. But why should the *Spectator* fix on the particular million in question, when a penny in the pound added to the income-tax would be more than sufficient? Evidently because in his eyes, all sinking-funds, however unassailable logically, are of no real value: because those funds, established again and again in England and France, have ended in nothing. He can admire the discharge of debt in the United States, and the vast project of discharging it all within a generation; but the very name of an English sinking-fund carries his mind to Utopia. Such, I believe, are the sentiments of most educated men.

Statistical Society neglects. A confirmation of this fact is found in the transactions of the *Statistical Society;* which is carried on principally by men who are the first to recognise the value of such a proceeding as a sinking-fund: by leading actuaries, secretaries of insurance companies, permanent heads of Government offices, with a few amateurs. Now in the *Statistical Journal*, there are abundant papers on Mortality, Crime, Education, Taxation, Wages, and Indian Affairs, but scarcely anything about payment of the National Debt.

Why is the public indifferent? It is easy to understand why the public has no affection for a sinking-fund, which means, in the first instance, increased taxation: when we are told in Parliament and in the newspapers, that all such efforts have failed, and in the nature of things will fail, we inevitably draw back from useless increased taxation: we have come to regard all such projects as means for drawing money out of our pockets under false pretences.

IV.

Why are the leaders of opinion indisposed?

LET us now see the arguments on which the leaders of opinion have relied. Mr. McCulloch was lately regarded as a high authority, and he thus stated his opinion.*

McCulloch. "For upwards of twenty years this pitiful juggle was kept up; Parliament and the nation believing, notwithstanding the most decisive experience to the contrary, that it was rapidly diminishing the public debt! Dr. Hamilton, of Aberdeen, had the merit of dissipating this delusion, the grossest, certainly, that ever imposed on any people. He showed, in his work on the National Debt, published in 1813, that the sinking-fund, instead of diminishing, had really added to the debt; and he proved to demonstration, that the excess of revenue above expenditure is the only sinking-fund by which any part of the National Debt can ever be discharged."

But Hamilton himself. That the latter part of this statement is true I do not dispute: debt can be paid only by saving in the first instance; though, as I have shown in the case of a private person, the time when the saving is effected is a matter of the highest importance. As to the former part of the sentence, let Dr. Hamilton speak for himself.†

"In regard to increase of taxes, we are of opinion that the sinking-fund *has had a real effect* in calling forth exertions, which, although they *might* have been made as well and as effectually, *would not* have

---

* McCulloch's "Adam Smith." 1839, 618.

† Hamilton's "Inquiry as to the National Debt." 1813, 153.

been made, unless to follow out the line which that system required. A loan is made, and the revenue considered as charged, not only with the interest, but a certain proportion of the principal, annually. *Taxes are imposed* to meet the one as well as the other. If the sinking-fund had not been in view, it is likely taxes would have been imposed for the interest only.

"If the sinking-fund could be conducted without loss to the public, or even if it were attended with a moderate loss, it would not be wise to propose an alteration of a system which has gained the confidence of the public, and which points out a rule of taxation that has the advantage, at least, of being steady. If that rule be laid aside, our measures of taxation might become entirely loose.

"But if the loss attending the sinking-fund be great (and the foregoing computation evinces that it has been so) it seems proper to inquire whether a plan might be followed that would deliver us from this loss, and at the same time carry on the necessary measure of increased taxation. The present proportion of one per cent. on the nominal capital might be continued; not, perhaps, as the most eligible, but as possessing the advantage of being established. If a loan of 20 millions be transacted in the Three per Cents., the sinking-fund attached to it, on the present system, is £333,333. Now taxes may be imposed to that extent, besides what are required for interest; and that sum, instead of being made over to commissioners, may be deducted from the loans. Thus, the nation would save the loss it at present sustains, of borrowing on lower, and paying on higher terms; the imposition of £333,333 additional taxes, which is the only measure of real efficiency, would be the same as before."

Hamilton's apparent contradiction. Before comparing these statements made by McCulloch and Hamilton, I will explain an apparent contradiction. Hamilton was unwilling to give up the actual system of taxation in connection with the sinking-fund; and only recommended the abandonment of the Commission because it caused a loss to the public. But if it caused a loss, why was he unwilling to abandon it?

Illustrated by a recent proceeding. A recent financial operation will explain this. A few years ago, Mr. Gladstone, as Chancellor of the Exchequer, wanting to borrow a considerable sum, and being unwilling to permanently increase the debt, proposed to grant terminable annuities, instead of the ordinary perpetual annuities. Mr. Hubbard afterwards calculated the result, and explained to the House of Commons, that this was an improvident measure: that in borrowing on terminable annuities, the country paid a higher rate of interest than in adding to the Three per Cents. Mr. Gladstone had not pretended that he borrowed at a lower rate on terminable annuities: what he proposed was to secure a sinking-fund; and whether, knowing the loss, he would repeat such a proposal, is another question.

Now, Mr. Hubbard, in showing that this loan on terminable annuities was borrowed at a high rate, did not express any opinion of the propriety of establishing a sinking-fund: he only complained of the loss occasioned by this mode of borrowing. A friend to sinking-funds might join with an enemy to them, in denouncing the improvidence of this particular loan. The friend to sinking-funds might say to Mr. Gladstone: I quite approve of your arranging for the extinction of this debt by a sinking-fund; but I object to your scheme of terminable annuities, because this is a dear way of doing it; because by doing it directly you would do it at less cost, and because therefore, your mode *causes a loss* to the public.

Hamilton's real meaning. This was exactly Hamilton's meaning. He approved of the sinking-fund: he conceded that its existence led to increased taxation; but he maintained that its actual form was not the best; and as in another form it would be carried on far more cheaply, he pronounced that the actual operations caused a loss to the public.

His recommendation. Hamilton did not recommend that the sinking-fund should be abandoned. He said that it had produced a real effect in calling forth exertions which would not otherwise have been made; and that if the country should abandon the rule, on each fresh loan, of adding to the taxation specifically for the sinking-fund, "our measures of taxation might become entirely loose." What he did recommend was this:—that the separate establishment of sinking-fund commissioners and their accounts, should be abolished; and that the additional sums previously raised by taxation, should still be raised, and should be at once deducted from the loans.

In time of war. It must be remembered that he wrote during the war, and towards the close of that interminable war which made loans inevitable and immense. Yet even under these most adverse circumstances, he still advised that the sinking-fund should be continued, but in a different form: just as Mr. Hubbard might advise Mr. Gladstone, not to abandon the project of diminishing the National Debt, but to effect it directly, instead of indirectly.

McCulloch's error. We can now estimate the value of Mr. McCulloch's censures: he said that the sinking-fund was a "pitiful juggle;" that it was a "delusion, the grossest, certainly, that ever imposed on any people:" and that Dr. Hamilton had the merit of dissipating that delusion, by proving that the sinking-fund, "instead of diminishing, had really added to the debt." Dr. Hamilton, as I have shown, did not regard the sinking-fund as a pitiful juggle, or a delusion: he did not contend that it had added to the debt: he did not recommend its abolition. He held, on the contrary, that the sinking-fund had caused increased taxation and a diminution of debt: he only proved that the form was not the best possible, and that by a change of that form the diminution of debt would be more effectually carried out: he recommended that the sums obtained as a sinking-fund, instead of being invested in the hands of commissioners, should be deducted from loans raised.

Lord Grenville on Hamilton. Mr. McCulloch cannot have troubled himself to read Dr. Hamilton: he must have known him only at second-hand. Now Lord Grenville who has the credit of giving the fatal blow to the system, did know what Dr. Hamilton recommended, and did express his own disagreement.*

"With respect to the distinguished writer whom I have named, there are *not a few* of the topics on which I have most dwelt, as well as some others which I have not had occasion so particularly to notice in this essay, respecting which his opinons, if I rightly apprehend them, differ, I regret to say it, very much from mine."

When we find such carelessness in a laborious compiler of statistical works, we cannot be surprised at misapprehension on the part of men generally. A recent debate in the House of Commons, furnishes examples.

---

* 2nd Edition. 1828, vii. viii.

V.

House of Commons debate, 4th April, 1867, on S. F. ON the 4th April, 1867, Mr. Disraeli brought forward his budget, and adopted in it Mr. Gladstone's plan of the previous year, for getting rid of a considerable amount of debt. The discussion that followed well exhibits the ordinary sentiments of educated men.

Sir G. Bowyer, Sir George Bowyer, though he has written a good deal, and though he is a distinguished defender of the faith he has adopted, has probably not paid any particular attention to financial topics; and therefore fairly represents the predominant notions of highly educated men, few of whom, in England, do turn their attention to finance, unless compelled by the necessities of politics.

condemned it. Sir George* objected to the plan for the reduction of the National Debt, as he had objected to it in 1866. " The plan was *nothing more than that of a sinking-fund.* When the £24,000,000 was wiped off at the end of 18 years, there would be a surplus created of something more than £1,500,000, but we had got very nearly that now, so that the thing was as broad as it was long. As to our public credit, he thought that if we had to go into the market, we should have a better chance of making good terms if we could say that we had a million surplus, than we should have if we told borrowers that, at the end of 18 years, £24,000,000 of our National Debt would be extinguished. . . . . In the event of a war breaking out, the Chancellor of the Exchequer would not be able to borrow

---

* *Times,* 5th April, 1867; p. 6, col. 6.

money more advantageously than if these prospective reductions had not been determined on ; but, on the contrary, he would then have reason to regret that he had pledged himself to this increased annuity. Indeed the scheme was worse than the old sinking-fund, which might be given up at any time, and the surplus revenue taken. In the present instance, however, a pledge was made to give up the surplus revenue for 18 years, and even if a war broke out, the arrangement could not be changed."

The leading idea in these remarks is, I believe, that the old sinking-fund was, beyond all question, bad ; and that not in form only, but even in substance. The scheme now on foot is condemned, first, because it is nothing more than a sinking-fund ; and secondly, because it is worse even than the old sinking-fund.

Mr. Hubbard. Mr. Hubbard followed, and also condemned the proposed plan. His career as a London merchant and bank director, has so far modified his opinions, that he refrained from absolutely condemning an attempt to diminish the debt : but he showed the faintness of his desire to do it, by declaring that so long as the duty on fire insurances is not again considerably reduced, the reduction of the National Debt ought to be postponed.

As Editor of "Spectator." I showed before that the *Spectator* suggested the re-arming our forces at the expense of this proposed fund : Mr. Hubbard would reduce the fire insurance duty at the expense of the proposed fund : a penny in the pound added to the income-tax would accomplish both purposes. The *Spectator* and Mr. Hubbard agree in estimating at a very low rate the duty of reducing the National Debt.

Mr. Laing. I am more surprised to see the same side taken by Mr. Laing ; whose course of life as a distinguished mathematician, railway chairman, and Indian finance minister, should have set him free from ordinary prejudices. In the debate of the 4th April, he suggested a postponement for further consideration; though a year's previous postponement would seem enough for any man. But his subsequent remarks showed his real disinclination to all sinking-funds. He said that the nation, like an individual landowner, "might adopt either of two principles. It might either better its condition by paying off the National Debt by instalments; or, continuing the payment of interest, it might apply all surplus revenues to the improvement of the estate. For a long series of years the latter principle had been the one pursued. In the words used by the late Lord Sydenham, then Mr. Powlett Thomson, 'the money was left to fructify in the pockets of the people.'"

Did it not occur to Mr. Laing that there were not two, but three ways of applying a certain individual revenue? First, it might be applied to pay off a part of the principal of the national debt: secondly, as Mr. Laing says, it might be saved by the owner, and capitalized: thirdly, it might be finally spent by the owner. Mr. Laing assumes that the money left in the taxpayer's pocket, will be saved, and used productively. But he should remember that far the greater part of men's incomes is spent. Even during the late prosperity, before the commercial crash of 1866, it was calculated that out of an aggregate income of 600 or 700 millions, the saving was only 130 or 150 millions; and this was regarded as an immense amount. In the same proportion, if it were proposed to levy a million a year for a sinking-fund, and instead of this the million was left to fructify in the people's pockets, the accumulation would be, not a million, but only one-fifth of that sum.

Conclusion so far; as to the public, We see then, why the public looks askance at a sinking-fund: it does not like the taxation necessary for it; and it is told by most of its leaders that the taxation would be wasted. It paid cheerfully, the sixteenpence income-tax to sustain the national honour in the Crimean war; but it grudges a penny income-tax to raise the national credit. The public is so far right; for in a matter that has been rendered so complex as this, it must take its opinions from its leaders: it can no more be its own financier, than each man can be his own lawyer or his own physician.

and as to the leaders. If the political leaders are generally wrong, as I believe they are, there is less excuse for them. They have no right to take their opinions from writers even of reputation: they are bound to judge for themselves. It is a consolation however, to find such eminent exceptions as Sir G. C. Lewis, Mr. Gladstone, and Mr. Disraeli: men who have had their eyes opened by dealing with the facts of the annual budget.

VI.

Modern prosperity. PART of this national and political apathy, probably the greater part, is traceable to the remarkable course of events during the present century: to the rapid increase of population, and the still more rapid accumulation of wealth. Since 1815 the English population has doubled and the English wealth has probably trebled. As a consequence, the credit of the British Government has risen so high that the rate of interest on the debt has been reduced to a very low point. The principal of the debt is less than it was in 1815; the interest, which was more than 32 millions in 1815, is now only 26 millions, including the terminable annuities. We forget how heavily taxation pressed on us in 1815; that it was as though we had now to pay 100 millions a year for interest on the debt, instead of one-fourth of that amount. If our debt had grown to 2,000 millions, and our interest to 100 millions, we should have heard abundant outcry as to the necessity of reducing both. A sinking-fund would have been the text of many political discourses.

Will it last? We are so accustomed to the wonders of recent industrial successes, that we cease to ask how long this prosperity is to continue. We have been lately startled by a statement that our coal, the basis of our manufacturing success, is in a way to be exhausted. Whether this is true or not, it is certainly the dictate of wisdom, that during prosperity we should prepare for adverse circumstances. England would no doubt, continue to be a very considerable country, even if its manufacturing predominance ceased; as it was a considerable country before that manufacturing predominance existed. Its land and its agricultural skill, with the security attending its orderly but free government, must keep it in the first rank of European nations. But a failure of manufactures, and therefore of commerce, would involve a diminishing population, a falling revenue, and a pressure of taxation. If that time should come, I fear that our posterity would curse the apathy of their progenitors, who at a trifling sacrifice to themselves, might have made such arrangements as to wipe off the debt they had incurred.

VII.

Supposed con-fiscation of sinking-fund in war time.

SOME persons imagine that to maintain a sinking-fund is impossible;* for that even if it were established during peace, it would be confiscated for war purposes on the breaking out of hostilities. But this objection is founded apparently on a vague notion that a sinking-fund consists of something that either is tangible property, or that can be converted into tangible property. Now a sinking-fund is only a surplus of taxation beyond expenditure, formally applied to the reduction of debt: the sinking-fund of 1716 pretended to nothing more: that of 1786 attempted to add the application of compound interest; so that a million £ of surplus taxation applied this year, should accumulate at compound interest, and amount in 14, 18, or 20 years to 2 millions £: both these sinking-funds diminished the debt. It is true that on the breaking out of war, and the consequent raising of loans, as the surplus taxation ceased, the operation of the sinking-fund ceased in reality if not in name. But there was no confiscation; there was only cessation: so far as the sinking-fund acted, it diminished debt and that was all.

---

* They may quote the authority of Adam Smith (V. III. pa. 418 Ed. 1839), who says that a sinking-fund is certain "to be misapplied towards defraying all the extraordinary expenses which occur in times of peace." But he founds this opinion on another: that in times of peace, a people will not submit to a new tax. He wrote just before 1786, the year in which Pitt established his sinking-fund, and provided a million a year of surplus taxation to food it: this fund, as we shall see, was carried on in good faith, so long as peace continued. If Adam Smith therefore, had written ten years later, his opinions would have been qualified by his own experience. Probably Pitt, who was a disciple of Adam Smith, acted partly under the advice of his master.

Reality of sinking-funds. That national debts can be diminished is proved by facts. To say nothing of the results of Mr. Pitt's scheme, our debt was diminished between 1727 and 1739, by 6 millions £, an amount perhaps as great as 50 or 100 millions £ would be now: after the conclusion of the Seven Years' War, between 1763 and 1775, our debt was again diminished by 6 millions £, an amount perhaps as great as 30 or 50 millions £ now: between 1815 and 1838 it was diminished by nearly 74 millions £, an amount perhaps as great as 150 millions £ would be in 21 years from the present time. In the United States the Federal Government has more than once paid off the whole of its debt, and at one time after having done this had a surplus income which it lent to the particular States, and is still owing by them. But the most remarkable example is that of Holland. According to M. Maurice Block,* the Dutch Government, between 1850 and 1861, paid off nearly 200 millions of florins; that is, taking the florin at 1s. 8½d., the sum paid off was nearly 1½ millions £ a year; a sum as great as 11 or 12 millions a year would have been for us. The table given by M. Block,† for the longer period, 1847-61, makes the reduction of debt only about a million a year, or a sum as great as 8 millions £ a year would have been for us. If for this longer period of 14 years, we had done our duty as the Dutch did theirs, we should have lessened our debt by 112 millions, instead of allowing it to grow to a rather higher amount than that of 1838. If we had done the same thing since 1838, our debt would now have been 550 millions instead of 800 millions £.

---

* "Puissance Comparée," Gotha, 1862., p. 99.   † Ib., p. 164.

In the face of these facts, it is trifling to talk of any impossibility in maintaining a sinking-fund; unless it should be whimsically maintained that to save by fits and starts is more efficacious than to save with system and regularity.

VIII.

CONCLUSIONS.

THE conclusions then, at which I arrive in this chapter are the following.

An efficient sinking-fund is not to be obtained by any trick of figures, but by an honest surplus of national income above national expenditure.

At the same time, the amount of sacrifice required from the ratepayers, depends very much on the time when the sacrifice is enforced : a sum less than the cost of a single year's war, levied now and left to accumulate at compound interest, would in a hundred years pay off our whole debt; the same sum levied a hundred years hence, would do little more than pay one year's present interest.

This fund however, ought to be so raised as not to diminish the productive powers of the country : if it were so raised as to render capital scarce, the national loss might be greater than the national gain. Since however, the sum would not be spent but would only change hands, and since it would not be half or perhaps a third of the annual savings of the nation, any fear of mischief in this way, seems to me futile.

The public distaste to a sinking-fund is accounted for principally by the failure of that of 1786, which was continued with modifications till 1829 : this failure, as I shall show afterwards, was not so decisive as we have been told; and it is altogether untrue that Dr. Hamilton condemned sinking-funds generally : the dreadful wars between 1793 and 1815 are responsible for the disappointment.

Besides this, we have become so familiar with debt, that we forget the great and incurable evil attached to it : we overlook the fact that in each generation we pay as much for interest as the amount of the principal, without thereby diminishing the debt : that since 1815 we have paid the debt nearly twice over.

I show that since 1838, the principal of our debt has not diminished : but that it is possible to reduce the amount, is proved by our own successful efforts in the reign of George II., and again between 1763 and 1775, between 1786 and 1793, between 1815 and 1838 : it is proved by the action of the United States' Federal Government formerly ; it is proved above all by the example of the Dutch, who have paid off in 14 or 15 years an amount so large that if we had made equal efforts, our debt would have been reduced by 250 millions £.

CHAPTER II.

HISTORY OF BRITISH SINKING FUNDS.

I.

IN my former chapter, I have recalled those first principles on which all repayment of debt must be founded. I have shown also, that the very name of a Sinking-Fund is become unpopular, and is regarded even by judicious men as a word of reproach; so that to pronounce any financial scheme to be a sinking-fund is to say that it is worse than utopian; that it is something like a swindle on the public.

I propose in the present chapter, to lay before my readers a brief history of past sinking-funds; that it may be seen by what means these notions arose, and how far they are well founded.

II.

Origin of our debt: OUR ancestors till towards the close of the Stuart dynasty, knew nothing of a National Debt: the King owed money which he had spent for private or for public purposes; but the credit of the nation was not pledged for repayment. In 1688, the whole national debt was little more than half a million.

after 1688. During the reign of William and Mary*

---

* Mc.Culloch's " Adam Smith " 1839. 619.

however, large loans were contracted for carrying on the war against Louis XIV.; by 1702 the debt had increased to 16 millions; and since at that time it was as difficult to raise 5 millions of taxes as it would now be to raise 100 millions, a debt of 16 millions was a very considerable one.

Queen Anne. But the War of the Succession, ending in the Peace of Utrecht, led Queen Anne and her Parliament to borrow still more largely: at the close of her reign the nation owed 54 millions. There was an audacity in the proceeding which resembled the recent one of the United States in borrowing an amount ten times as great.

In the eyes of the nation, excepting the Jacobite minority, the money was well spent: for though the Peace of Utrecht was believed to have weakly given up the advantages we had gained, and to have shamefully abandoned our allies the Catalans, yet the effect of the whole war was to reduce the French nation to the utmost distress, and to so quell its restless spirit that for eighty subsequent years Europe was free from French dictation.

However audaciously a debt has been incurred, the interest must be paid; and the finance minister must have looked with dismay at the necessity of providing $3\frac{1}{4}$ millions, which was the annual charge. To us this appears a small sum, but it was a large proportion of the public revenue, which at the beginning of the eighteenth century was only 5 millions, and which was thought to have increased wonderfully, when, during the reign of George II., it reached $8\frac{1}{2}$ millions.*

The alarm that was felt lest the nation should be unable to bear this heavy burden, and lest its credit

---

* Leone Levi, "Taxation" 15.

should be so impaired that future war loans would
be impossible, led to the establishment of our first
sinking-fund : and so steadily and honestly was this
fund managed, that during the years between 1721
and 1738, the debt instead of being increased, was
diminished by 8 millions, while the annual interest
was diminished by one-fourth.

III.

Sinking-fund 1716: Dr. Price's account. SINKING-FUNDS are no new invention : Adam Smith* speaks of one in Holland in 1655, and of another in the
Ecclesiastical State in 1685. A French writer however,† seems to attribute the invention to us. As to
the measure of 1716, Dr. Price‡ gives the following
account.

"The sinking-fund was established in the year
1716, or soon after the accession of the present
family, at a time when the public debts, though not
much more than a third of what they are now,** were
thought to be so considerable as to be alarming and
dangerous. It was intended as a SACRED DEPOSIT
never to be touched; the law which established it
declaring, that it was to be applied to the payment
of the principal and interest of such national debts
and incumbrances, as had been incurred before the
25th of *December*, 1716; *and to no other use, intent,
or purpose whatever.*— The faith of *Parliament*,
therefore, as well as the security of the kingdom,

---

* " A. Smith," v. iii. pa. 418 of ed. 1839.   † *Dict. de l'Écon. Pol.*
Vol. I. 684. 2.   ‡ Price, "Reversionary Payments," 4th ed. I. 208.
** That is before the debt contracted for the American war. Dr. Price
wrote on the subject first in 1772. (Hamilton 1813 pa. 98.)

seemed to require, that it should be preserved carefully and rigorously from alienation. But, notwithstanding this, it has been *generally* alienated; and the produce of it employed, in helping to defray such current expenses as the exigencies of the state rendered necessary.

"In order to justify this, it has been usual to plead, that when money is wanted, it makes no difference, whether it is taken from hence, or procured by making a new loan. But in truth the difference between these two methods of procuring money is no less than *infinite*. For by employing the SINKING-FUND in bearing current expenses rather than borrowing *new* money or new funds; the state, in order to avoid giving *simple interest* for money, is made to alienate money, that *must* have otherwise been improved at *compound interest:* and which, in time, would have *necessarily* increased to *any* sum. Had a faithful use been made from the first, of only one THIRD of the produce of this fund, the greatest part of our present debts would now have been discharged."

His fundamental notions. This quotation exhibits Dr. Price's leading notions: first, that a nation should borrow at simple interest, and accumulate a sinking-fund at compound interest; secondly, that when the Government has to procure funds beyond the produce of the taxes, the necessary sum should be borrowed rather than taken from the sinking-fund. I will postpone further consideration of these two propositions till my next chapter; because I have undertaken in this chapter to supply only a history of facts and opinions.

Dr. Hamilton's account. Dr. Hamilton in his account is, naturally, free from that enthusiasm which distinguishes Dr. Price; who when writing, thought himself the first inventor of the sinking-fund at compound interest; though he afterwards candidly confessed that he had found himself anticipated, in a pamphlet of 1726, which had reached at least four editions.*

"SIR ROBERT WALPOLE'S SINKING-FUND.

" The first plan for the discharge of the National Debt, formed on a regular system, and conducted for some time with a considerable degree of firmness, was that of the sinking-fund, established in 1716, under the administration of Sir Robert Walpole. The taxes which had been laid on before for limited periods, being rendered perpetual, and distributed among the *South Sea, Aggregate, and General Funds*, as has been mentioned already,† and the produce of these funds being greater than the charges upon them, the surplusses were united under the name of the *sinking-fund*, being appropriated for the discharge of the National Debt. The legal interest had been reduced from six to five per cent. above two years before, and as that reduction was conformable to the commercial state of the country, Government was now able to obtain the same reduction on the interest of the public debt, and apply the savings in aid of the sinking-fund. In 1727, a further reduction of the interest of the public debt from five to four per cent. was obtained, by which nearly £400,000 was added to the sinking-fund. And in the year 1749, the interest of part of the debt was again reduced to three and a half per cent. for seven years, and to three per cent. thereafter ; and in 1750, the interest

---

* Price, " Reversionary Payments." 1. 209.
† Hamilton's Inquiry. 1813. 95. ‡ Ib. pa. 67.

of the remainder was reduced to three and a half per cent. for five years, and to three per cent. thereafter, by which a further saving of near £600,000 was added to the sinking-fund.

"The opinion, strongly urged since by Dr. Price, seems to have been entertained at that time, of the importance of applying the produce of the sinking-fund invariably to the discharge of the National Debt, or borrowing by new loans when the public exigencies required it. Accordingly the following sums were borrowed towards the supplies, from 1718 to 1731, being a period of peace.

In 1718	£505,995
„ 1719	312,737
„ 1720	500,000
„ 1721	1,000,000
„ 1722	
„ 1723	
„ 1724	
„ 1725	500,000
„ 1726	370,000
„ 1727	1,750,000
„ 1728	1,230,000
	6,168,732
In 1729	£550,000
„ 1730	1,200,000
„ 1731	500,000
	8,418,732

"The sums applied from the sinking-fund to the discharge of the National Debt, from 1716 to 1728, amounted to £6,648,000, being a very little more than the additional debt contracted in that time.

"In 1728, the sinking fund was charged with the interest of the loan, and this was also done in the loans of the following years, and *the additional taxes imposed* for the payment of the interest of the loans, were applied directly to that fund.

"Soon after, the plan of preserving the sinking

fund inviolate, and borrowing by new loans, was abandoned. In 1733, £500,000 was taken from the sinking-fund towards the supplies of the year. In 1734, £1,200,000 was taken from it for the same purpose; and in 1735. it was anticipated and mortgaged. Since that time, the operations of the sinking-fund, in time of peace, have been feeble, its produce being often diverted to other purposes: and at that time, the nation had no other free* revenue, except the annual land and malt taxes, which were inadequate to the expense of a peace establishment on the most moderate scale. It was therefore necessary to have recourse to the sinking-fund, or to the inefficient system of discharging old debts and contracting new ones. In the peace which followed the treaty of Utrecht, being a period of 26 years, the longest which the nation ever enjoyed, the amount of debt discharged was only £7,328,355. In time of war its produce was applied to the service of the year, and loans only made for the additional sums wanted.

"The produce of the sinking fund at its commencement, in 1717, was £323,439

Medium annual produce, from 1717 to 1726, both inclusive	577,614
1727 to 1736..................	1,132,251
1737 to 1746...:...............	1,062,170
1747 to 1756..................	1,356,578
1757 to 1766..................	2,059,406
1767 to 1776..................	2,584,250

---

* By free revenue is meant, I believe, a revenue not pledged for payment of interest of a particular loan. At that time, and long afterwards, the Government when it borrowed, pledged some permanent tax for payment of the interest; just as Mexico or Turkey now borrows, and pledges the custom duties for the interest. The free revenue was the revenue not so pledged. This explains the term *funds*, about which Cobbett made himself merry: people, he said, imagined the existence of a strong box in which these funds were locked up; and they had no notion that the funds had been already spent. But so long as a loan was contracted on the pledge of a specific tax, the funds meant, the proceeds of the tax so hypothecated.

"It seems unnecessary to trace the operations of this sinking-fund further. It was continued nominally in the accounts of the exchequer, until the establishment of Mr. Pitt's sinking-fund in 1786, but did little in time of peace, and nothing in time of war, to the discharge of the national debt. Dr. Price says, that at the time he wrote, in 1772, it had afforded about 20 millions towards the payment of the national debt in 56 years, being nearly £357,000 annually, at an average. If from this sum of 20 millions, we subtract the debt contracted from 1716 to 1728, the remainder is nearly equal to the debts discharged in the periods of peace which followed the treaties of Utrecht and Aix-la-Chapelle."

Price and Hamilton compared. It will be seen that Dr. Price and Dr. Hamilton differ much in the spirit which animates them: Dr. Price regards the sinking-fund as a SACRED DEPOSIT; Dr. Hamilton analyses it with the coolness of a professor.

Price and Grenville compared. Dr. Price and Lord Grenville differ no less. Lord Grenville attributes the alienation of the fund to the sagacity of Sir Robert Walpole. "The ministers," he says,* "frequently supported their sinking-fund by borrowed surpluses, and this not in war only, but in peace. They seem to have thought it no contradiction to increase debt in the very moments of professing to reduce it. But so great an inconsistency did not long escape the sagacity of Walpole; a minister, who, in some other instances, no less than in this, seems not a little to have outrun the wisdom of his contemporaries. By measures which, notwithstanding all the clamour of his opponents, it would be very difficult to censure on any just ground of reasoning,

---

* Grenville, Essay, 1828, 16.

he diverted the sinking-fund from these unreal and simulated operations."

Dr. Price's view of the alienation is singularly different from this.* "From some publications in 1726 it appears that some persons had been led to apprehend this zeal of the ministry would not be permanent, because it was not their interest to pay off the public debt, on account of the dependence and influence created by it. In answering this objection, the writers on the side of the court called such an apprehension *an indecent jealousy*, and took upon them to assure the public, ' that in no possible exigence of affairs could our ministers ever approve of or recommend the alienation of the *sinking-fund*.' Happy would it have been for *Britain* had this proved true : BUT in a little time it appeared, that the apprehensions which had been styled *indecent jealousies*, were too well grounded. Men in power came soon to see, that this *fund* was advancing too fast in its operations, and to change their zeal for it into a resolution to destroy it."

Over-refine-ments. Both Lord Grenville and Dr. Price seem to me to have given over-refined reasons for a plain matter. Lord Grenville regards Sir Robert Walpole's proceedings as the result of extraordinary financial sagacity : Dr. Price regards them as the result of a fear that the nation should too soon get out of debt. I fancy that if Sir Robert had anticipated such assertions, a horse-laugh would have been his reply.

Walpole's alleged sagacity. Walpole was, no doubt, a very sagacious statesman : the aim of his policy was to keep the Jacobites from upsetting the settlement of the crown on the Brunswick line : to do

---

* " Reversionary Payments." 1783. I. 216.

this it was highly important to avoid irritating the country with heavy taxes. This explains why in 1733,* when, "in order to keep the land tax at one shilling in the pound, it was necessary either to borrow half a million for the current service, or to take half a million from the sinking-fund, the last method was chosen." Probably a wise proceeding; but the sagacity was political, not financial.

Alleged fears of extinction of debt. As to Dr. Price's explanation, that Walpole and his friends feared to see the nation out of debt, some proof should have been offered of the existence of alarms so unusual. Many nations have repudiated their debts: many have partially repudiated them by arbitrarily lowering the interest: I never heard of an authenticated instance of national lamentation over the disappearance of debt.

Explanation. The entire proceedings seem to me simple. After the peace of Utrecht, the novelty of a large public debt caused great alarm: the Patriots proclaimed national ruin: the Whigs feared that if war broke out again, the exhaustion which had actually overtaken France, would be our fate too. The debt must be diminished. The sinking-fund therefore was established. As the result, the principal payed off was not very great; but the return of prosperity and public credit enabled the Government to lower the rate of interest, just as happened a century later, after the battle of Waterloo had wound up the Napoleonic drama. From 6 per cent. the rate was reduced to 5, 4, and long afterwards to 3: and the annual charge fell between 1713 and 1738 from 3 millions to 2 millions. Our annual charge has fallen from 32 millions to 26: the fears which

---

* Price's "Reversionary Payments." 1783. 217.

oppressed us in 1816 have ceased. The nation then, like the nation now, was unwilling to be taxed for further reduction of the debt. There is no need to resort to further explanations; neither to the extraordinary financial sagacity of Walpole, nor to the indecent jealousies of politicians.

IV.

1716 to 1786. DURING the seventy years that followed 1716, nothing new was done. A thinker here and there may have grumbled at the national carelessness which failed to diminish the debt, and after 1741 much increased it. I have mentioned the candour of Dr. Price in confessing that a pamphet of 1726, which went through several editions, anticipated his scheme of a fund at compound interest.

1727 to 1763, and to 1775. Any large addition to the debt, seems generally followed by a cry for a sinking-fund. During the reign of George II. there was such an addition; for including the three first years of George III., during which time the seven years' war was concluded, the debt rose from 52 millions to 132 millions. Yet there was no new sinking fund. That of 1716 however, still kept its place in the accounts of the exchequer: efforts were actually made to reduce the debt; and in the twelve years ending with 1775, there was paid off no less than 6 millions.

1775 to 1784. Then, unfortunately, broke out the war with the American colonies; which cost us vast sums unprofitably spent, and left us with a debt of 245 millions: a sum nearly twice as great as that of 1763, and nearly five times as great as that of 1727.

The annual charge was comparatively low; for it was only 9½ millions, or less than 4 per cent.; whereas in 1714, on the small amount of 36 millions, it had been above 8 per cent.

National discouragement: Adam Smith. The nation however, was greatly discouraged by its failure to conquer the Americans; by its loss of old colonies; and by the extravagant debt it had incurred. Even the philosophical Adam Smith, who clearly saw the fallacies of the colonial system, appears to have felt humiliated at the reduction of the empire; just as many philosophers among ourselves would feel, if our Indian possessions were suddenly torn from us. The following are the last sentences of the "Wealth of Nations," which was published at the opening of the war.

"If the colonies, notwithstanding their refusal to submit to British taxes, are still to be considered as provinces of the British empire, their defence in some future war may cost Great Britain as great an expense as it ever has done in any former war. The rulers of Great Britain have, for more than a century past, amused the people with the imagination that they possessed a great empire on the west side of the Atlantic. This empire, however, has hitherto existed in imagination only. It has hitherto been, not an empire, but the project of an empire; not a gold mine, but the project of a gold mine; a project which has cost, which continues to cost, and which, if pursued in the same way as it has been hitherto, is likely to cost immense expense, without being likely to bring any profit; for the effects of the monopoly of the colony trade, it has been shown, are to the great body of the people, mere loss instead of profit. It is surely now time that our rulers should either realise this golden dream, in which they have been indulging themselves, perhaps, as well as the people, or that they should awake from it themselves, and endeavour to awaken the people. If the project cannot be completed, it ought to be given up. If any of the provinces of the British empire cannot be made to contribute towards the support of the whole empire, it is surely time that Great Britain should free herself from the expense of defending those provinces in time of war, and of supporting any part of their civil or military establishments in time of peace, and endeavour to *accommodate her future views and designs to the real mediocrity of her circumstances.*

This was written at least seven years before the conclusion of peace; and it seems that Adam Smith regarded the probable loss of the colonies as a reduction of the empire to a mediocrity of circumstances, and as a humiliating necessity. We may guess how it must have been felt by other men of a less disciplined character, or who believed that the colonies were a source of profit. The war went on, until the European aid given to the Americans made the struggle hopeless; and the French, whom we had turned out of Canada twenty years before, saw us turned out of New England and New York and Virginia, and all the thirteen provinces.

General resolution to lessen the debt. The debt would have been heavy enough if it had been accompanied with success: with failure added it could hardly be borne. There was an outcry for a reduction: not by repudiation or unjust lowering of interest, but by repayment of principal. So obvious was the necessity of doing something, that it was unnecessary to prove it. Mr. Pitt* "began with

---

* Annual Register, "Hist. Europe," 1786. 114.

observing, that the necessity we were under of adopting some means or other for the diminution of our National Debt, was a point upon which all persons and parties were universally agreed."

Dr. Price, 1773. Dr. Price, as early as 1773, had urged the dangerous condition of a nation which was always borrowing and never paying.* "The practice of raising the necessary supplies for every national service, by borrowing money on interest, to be continued till the principal is discharged, must be in the highest degree detrimental to a kingdom, unless a plan is settled, for putting its debts into a regular and certain course of payment. When this is not done, a kingdom by such a practice, obliges itself to return for every sum it borrows, infinitely greater sumss and, for the sake of a present advantage, subject, itself to a burden which must be always growing heavier and heavier, till it becomes insupportable.

"This seems to be now the very state of this nation. At the REVOLUTION, an era in other respects truly glorious, the practice I have mentioned began. Ever since, the public debt has been increasing fast, and every new war has added much more to it, than was taken from it during the preceding period of peace. . . . . . No resources can be sufficient to support a kingdom long in such a course. 'Tis obvious, that the consequence of accumulating debts so rapidly; and of mortgaging posterity, and funding for eternity, in order to pay the interest of them; must in the end prove destructive. Rather than go on in this way, it is absolutely necessary, that no money should be borrowed, except on annuities, which are to termi-

---

* Reversionary Payments, 1783, 1. 181.

nate* within a given period. Were this practised, there would be a LIMIT beyond which the national debts could not increase ; and time would do that *necessarily* for the public, which, if trusted to the œconomy of the conductors of its affairs, might possibly *never* be done."

Apology for Dr. Price. In order to do justice to Dr. Price, the whole of his opinions ought to be taken into account. If the population of Great Britain had been stationary, the progress of the debt would have been ruinous. Let us look again at the amounts of principal and interest.†

	Principal.	Interest.	Annual Payments.
1689	£664,263	£30,855	say 40 thousand £
1702	£16,394,702	£1,310,942	say 1¼ millions.
1714	£54,145,363	£3,351,358	say 3¼ millions.
1763	£138,865,430	£4,852,051	say 5 millions.

During the wars of William and Mary, an annual taxation of 5 millions was regarded as heavy : sixty years later the same 5 millions only paid the interest of the debt. With a stationary population such an augmentation of charges must have issued in national bankruptcy.

Population not really stationary. The population indeed, was not stationary. Nor did Dr. Price believe that it was stationary. He thought it was worse than this : he offered proof that it had diminished. He shared this error with many other thinkers : no thanks to the Bishops, who by their votes and influence in the House of Lords‡ had thrown out at the close of George the Second's

---

* Terminable annuities are still the favourite resource of speculative financiers. It is conceded however, that they are a very improvident form of sinking-fund, and open to precisely the objection made to Mr. Pitt's scheme, that of doing their work at the expense of a great loss to the nation. I will enter on this topic again.

† Mc Culloch's " Adam Smith." 1839. 619.

‡ Lord Colchester's Diary, 1. 84., says about the year 1753 or 1754.

reign, a bill for numbering the people. Price had taken pains to satisfy himself as to the facts; he had compared the deaths and baptisms of the town of Northampton: he had assumed erroneously, that all children born were baptised; and finding that the deaths outnumbered the baptisms, he concluded that Northampton was gradually being depopulated. This seems to us a slender foundation to rest on; just as a writer now would be deemed to build on a slender foundation, who told us that the population of Macclesfield is stationary, and therefore the population of England is stationary. I do not suppose however, that Price founded his own opinion on the Northampton facts: probably these only supported a foregone conclusion in his own mind, and furnished the means of impressing the public.

But if it had been. If population were stationary, the progress of the debt was alarming: if population were diminishing, bankruptcy was inevitable. Even with a diminishing population indeed, wealth may increase: we see now, that in an over-peopled country, a reduction of population is the very thing wanted to increase wealth; just as in a besieged town, to turn out the non-combatants adds to the resources of the defenders. But the theory of population was not then understood. It was not known that by the progress of civilization, and the consequent reduction of infant mortality, there had arisen a tendency in western Europe to over-population: it had not been discovered that the tendency to *depopulation*, which is still found among the Red Indians, and in parts of European Russia, had quite ceased among ourselves.

Actual increase. In 1801 the population of England was 9 millions: it is now more than 20 millions. Suppose that instead of more than doubling it had fallen to 8 or 7 millions. Dr. Price's vaticinations would have proved true: we could not have paid our debts and maintained our place among European nations. *Circumstances favoured us.* We are justly proud of being able to say, that since the Revolution, nearly two hundred years ago, the nation has never failed in its engagements; nor can it be denied that the fact is just matter for rejoicing: but we ought to remember that circumstances have favoured our sense of justice; and that without the growth of manufactures, naturally followed by the extension of commerce, and also of agriculture, we must have broken down under the burden of our debt. Dr. Price, on his own hypothesis of a decreasing population, was perfectly right.

V.

1786: *Pitt's sinking-fund: King's speech.* THE war with the American colonies then, and the vast additional debt caused by it, had driven the nation to resolve on a new sinking-fund: the King's speech prepared the Houses for an intended measure.
Committee appointed to investigate finances The Annual Register* gives the following statement. "Mr. Pitt had early in this session taken notice of that part of his Majesty's speech which related to the necessity of providing for the diminution of the National Debt; he had at the same time given the House to understand that such was the present flourishing condition of the revenue, that the annual national income would not only equal the annual

---

* Annual Register. " History of Europe." 1786. p. 111.

national disbursements, but would leave a surplus of considerable magnitude; this surplus, he said, he meant to form into a permanent fund, to be constantly and invariably applied to the liquidation of the public debt. In pursuance of this information to the House, and in order to ascertain the amount of the surplus in question, Mr. Pitt, previous to his entering into the state of the finances, or ways and means for the present year, moved, "That the several accounts and other papers presented that session, relating to the public income and expenditure, be referred to the consideration of a select committee, and that the said committee be directed to examine and report to the House, what might be expected to be the annual amount of the income and expenditure in future."

Their report. The committee presented this balance sheet.

RECEIPT.

	From Michaelmas 1784, to Michaelmas 1785.	From 5th January 1785, to 5th January 1736.
1 Total net payments into the Exchequer, from Michaelmas 1784 to Michaelmas 1785 .... £12,321,520		
Deduct therefrom the respited duties paid by East India Co. £401,118		
Excess beyond future amt. of window duties 46,189		
	447,307	11,874,213
1 Total net payments into the Exchequer, from 5th January 1785 to 5th January 1786 12,499,916		
The respited duties paid by East India Co. £401,118		
Excess beyond future amt. of window duties 56,101		
	457,219	12,042,697
2 Further produce of window duty imposed by the 24th George III.......................	380,056	253,534
3 Further produce of duty on two-wheel and four-wheel carriages	59,281	107,186
Carried forward............	£12,313,650	12,403,417

Brought forward......	£12,313,650	12,403,417
4 To complete (sic.) the former duty on male servants	26,803	42,444
5 Further produce of the duties on horses, wagons, and carts	56,829	73,610
6 Further produce of taxes imposed, 1784	103,000	22,000
7 Ditto ditto ditto, 1785, including the improvement of the medicine duty	265,000	242,000
8 Paid at the excise and alienation office, in part of civil list	14,000	14,000
9 Produce of the land and malt	2,600,000	2,600,000
	£15,379,182	15,397,471

EXPENDITURE.

10 Interest and charges of public debt	£9,275,769		
11 Exchequer bills	258,000		
12 Civil list	900,000		
13 Charges on aggregate fund	64,600		
14 Navy	1,800,000		
14 Ordnance, (sic.)	348,000		
14 Army, (sic.)	1,600,000		
15 Militia	91,000		
16 Miscellaneous services	74,274		
17 Appointed duties.......................	66.538		
		14,478,181	14,478,181
Annual surplus............		901,001	919,290

Results. It would be out of place here to analyse this Balance Sheet: but a recent Chancellor of the Exchequer might be excused some regrets, on finding that our present peace establishment for army and navy is six times as great as that of 1786: though, as Mr. Pitt said, " the committee, in calculating the expenses of the different services, had purposely gone *upon the largest and most expensive establishments*" (p. 114, col. 2); and that the estimate with respect to the navy, army, and ordnance, "was large and ample, as calculated for times of peace" (p. 115). On the other hand, the 9½ millions for interest and management of debt, was a far heavier burden, population and wealth considered, than our present 25 or 26 millions.

The account not a Budget but a general estimate. The committee's Balance Sheet is far more favourable than might have been expected, at the conclusion of a long war, carried on at a great distance, with a profusion then unexampled. But Mr. Pitt's speech explained that the balance sheet was not what we understand by a Budget: that it was only an estimate of what might probably be the *permanent* income and expenditure of the country if peace were maintained. Ample, he said, as were the amounts stated for military and naval expenses, "as calculated for times of peace, *and as they were to stand in future,* yet it fell infinitely short of what was *the actual expenditure* for those establishments for the present year, or what would be for *two or three years to come.* The effects of the late tedious and expensive war would be felt for some time longer; and the necessary claims it had left on the public purse were such as it was wise and politic to comply with. Thus, for instance, the naval half-pay and pension lists were unavoidably much increased, and a number of ships which were now on the stocks, were to be completed, in order to save the expense that had already been incurred by them, and which otherwise, from the total decay of the vessels, would be lost." There was a similar actual excess of expenditure in the army. Taking the two services together, "these exceedings above what was stated in the report as the amount of their permanent expenditure, was above £750,000." However, "this was a sum, which from its very nature would gradually diminish, and in time be reduced to nothing. Supposing it to last four years, it would then be equal to a sum of 3 millions." Mr. Pitt believed that this would be provided for without any fresh taxation; "such were the extraordinary resources of the country."

These estimates may have been well founded: England was feeling the results of that manufacturing and commercial prosperity which had for some time set in. But everything depended on the maintenance of peace. Pitt assumed that England would have no further wars for many years; nor is it any discredit to him that he did not foresee the French Revolution, the subversion of European order, and the genius of Napoleon. A few years afterwards we were hurried into hostilities with France, and for twenty years expended men and money to an extent never dreamed of by the wildest politician. The French Revolution spoilt all.

Additional taxation. Yet this effort appears to have done something, for it caused an increase of taxation. In order to make up the necessary annual amount for the proposed sinking-fund, Mr. Pitt at once levied a fresh tax on spirits, which with a slight addition from another source, was expected to realise £100,000 a year. This indeed, was a small sum even for that period. Bnt it is probable enough that in the absence of this project for paying off debt, the taxation might have been reduced, either at once, or before the French war broke out seven years later.

The measure proposed. Mr. Pitt then, proposed that "in order to insure the due application of this fund to its destined object" Parliament should "vest in a certain number of commissioners the full power of disposing of it in the purchase of stock for the public in their own names. These commissioners should receive the annual million by quarterly payments of £250,000 to be issued out of the exchequer before any other money, except the interest of the National Debt itself; by these provisions, the fund would be secured, and no deficiencies in the national revenues could affect it, but such must be separately provided for by Parliament.

The amount. "The accumulated compound interest on a million yearly, together with the annuities that would fall into that fund, would in 28 years amount to such a sum as would leave a surplus of four millions annually, to be applied if necessary to the exigencies of the state."

How obtained. The amount of terminable annuities that would fall in, is not given in this abridged report. It must have been considerable; for a million a year, with compound interest, would not produce anything near what is mentioned. If the rate of interest were 5 per cent., and the expenses of management were otherwise defrayed, the million a year would amount in about 14 years to 20 millions; in about 28 years to 60 millions: the interest on this, still at 5 per cent. would be 3 millions, against the 4 millions mentioned. Now it can hardly be supposed, if peace had continued, and if the credit of Government had been steadily improved by the operation of the proposed fund, that the rate of interest on public loans would have been 5 per cent. During the peace after 1763,* the three per cents. had ranged from 80 to 90; *i.e.*, the rate of interest was much under 4 per cent. Towards the close of the American war indeed, the three per cents. had fallen to 54; *i.e.*, the rate of interest was above $5\frac{1}{2}$ per cent. On the whole, it could not be expected that the average future rate would be so high as 5 per cent; and even if it should prove to be 5 per cent, the fund accumulated by a million a year, would at the end of about 28 years, yield 3 and not 4 millions. Therefore, the terminable annuities to fall in, must have formed a large part of the fund.

---

* McCulloch. "Commercial Dictionary." 1840. 589.

Mr. Pitt's accuracy not disputed. I do not mean to express doubts as to the accuracy of Mr. Pitt's calculations: they were explained to the House of Commons in the presence of Mr. Fox and his party, who constituted a very unfriendly opposition. That party however, was not remarkable for support of valuable administrative measures. Mr. Fox himself was a magnificent partisan, and not a legislator: he was desirous of repealing Lord Hardwicke's Marriage Act, because he feared that it would hinder a due increase of population: it was not he, but Mr. Pitt, who welcomed the advances of the French government, which resulted in the commercial treaty of this very year, 1786: it was Pitt, and not Fox, who studied and adopted the doctrines of Adam Smith. Mr. Pitt's calculations therefore, were not likely to receive intelligent investigation from Mr. Fox; and the liberal party out of doors, would probably be so pleased to see the adoption of the scheme of Dr. Price, an eminent dissenter of acknowledged financial ability, that they would conceal any doubts they might have as to the accuracy of these calculations.

The Commissioners. Mr. Pitt proposed to entrust the fund to Commissioners: and he said "he should endeavour to choose persons of such weight and character as corresponded with the importance of the Commission they were to execute. The Speaker of the House of Commons, the Chancellor of the Exchequer, the Master of the Rolls, the Governor and Deputy Governor of the Bank of England, and the Accountant General of the High Court of Chancery, were persons who, from their several situations, he should think highly proper to be of the number."

Mr. Pitt's recapitulation. Mr. Pitt concluded by the following recapitulation. "*First*, that the yearly income of the State exceeded the permanent level of its* expenditure, by a sum of £900,000. *Next*, that this sum would be increased to a million by means in no ways burthensome to the people. *Thirdly*, that although the present establishment exceeded in certain instances the same establishments as stated in the report of the select committee, yet there were ample resources, and contingent and outstanding receipts, sufficient to overbalance such excesses, without having recourse to any fresh taxes. *And lastly*, that the ways and means for the present year would be sufficient to furnish the supplies, together with the sum of £250,000, to be applied quarterly towards the establishment of a new fund; and after all, would leave a considerable balance to be carried to the next year."

Mr. Pitt's motion Mr. Pitt then moved, "That the sum of one million be annually granted to certain Commissioners, to be by them applied to the purchase of stocks, towards discharging the public debt of this country; which money shall arise out of the surplusses, excesses, and overplus moneys, composing the fund commonly called the sinking-fund."

Lord Grenville's support. Forty years later, Lord Grenville proposed the abolition of this fund. As a member of the House of Commons in 1786, and as brother of Lord Buckingham, he had highly approved of Pitt's propositions. In his pamphlet of 1827-8, he thought it necessary to apologise for his change of opinion: his rather haughty and inflexible† spirit unwillingly confessed that the experience of a long political life had compelled this variation in his opinions. " The writer‡ of these pages was himself

---

* This *ought* to have been "of its *peace* expenditure."
† Lord Stanhope's Pitt. 2. 122; 3. 52; 4. 115.   ‡ Essay. 1828. 2.

a party to the too sanguine hopes of those who framed and proposed that law; confidently believing it one of the greatest services which could then be rendered to their country. To that opinion he long adhered; and even, now, after the lapse of more than forty years, he feels it still painful to renounce so flattering a persuasion. But the interests of truth and science are paramount to all such considerations; and he who was formerly among the warmest advocates of a sinking-fund, is, on that account, the more strongly bound to avow, on every fit occasion, the distrust which he now entertains of its efficacy and real benefit. This is the true consistency of public duty."

Hamilton's account of the fund. Hamilton gives a concise account of this measure.*

"MR. PITT'S SINKING-FUND.

"The present sinking fund was established under Mr. Pitt's administration, in 1786. The various branches of revenue then existing were united under the name of the Consolidated Fund. One million taken from that fund was vested annually in the hands of Commissioners for the Redemption of the National Debt, to be applied for purchasing capital in such stocks as they should judge expedient, at the market prices. To this fund was to be added the interest of the debt redeemed and annuities fallen in by the failures of lives, or the expiring of the terms for which they were granted. When this fund amounted to four millions, it was enacted that the interest of the redeemed debt, and annuities fallen in, were no longer to be applied to it, but remain at the disposal of Parliament."

---

* Inquiry. 1813. 99.

Limitation to 4 millions. This limitation to four millions is highly approved by Lord Grenville :* "the principle of unlimited accumulation was expressly excluded from that law, by a provision which limited to four millions the sinking-fund then established. A wise precaution, showing an early and just apprehension of the evils since felt from an opposite policy." The limitation is also mentioned† by Lord Stanhope.

Lord Grenville's admission. I have mentioned that in Hamilton's opinion, the sinking-fund though it did not act so beneficially as it might have done, yet certainly reduced the debt, by causing increased taxation. Lord Grenville does not deny the increased taxation, though he strongly dissents ‡ from Hamilton's conclusions. He says§ that Mr. Pitt, "with an ardent and generous spirit, devoting all its energies to the national prosperity, risked, and in no small degree surrendered his highly valued popularity to the *necessity of the large additional taxation* which that measure compelled him to establish and to maintain. This was no light sacrifice, nor did he feel it as such." Lord Grenville does not tell us what became of the proceeds of this large additional taxation. Hamilton says it went in reduction of the debt.

Parliamentary objections, 1786. Mr. Pitt's measure met, of course, with opposition. ‖ Sir Grey Cooper, Mr. Fox, Mr. Sheridan, and Mr. Hussey, stated objections "to what they termed the insufficiency, and in some instances the impolicy, of the mode which Mr. Pitt had adopted to accomplish so great and so desirable an end.

---

* Essay. 1828., ix. † Life of Pitt, 1. 290.
‡ Grenville Essay, 1828. viii. § *Ib.* 20. ‖ Annual Regster, 1786, 117.

"These objections were of a two-fold nature: 1st, such as tended to show that the supposed excess of £900,000 in the national income over its expenditure, arose from false and mistaken calculations and conclusions in the report of the select committee, and such as the real state of the finances of the country by no means warranted : 2nd, such as went to the purposed mode of applying that excess or surplus, provided it existed. Mr. Sheridan subsequently moved resolutions to this effect; but they were negatived without a division."

Borrowing from the funds: proposed by Mr. Fox. In the opinion of many persons, the whole scheme was rendered valueless, by the practice which afterwards prevailed of making loans to the Government out of the sinking-fund. This arose at first from a proposal made by Mr. Fox, willingly acceded to however, by Mr. Pitt. "Mr. Fox, on the day for reconsidering the report of the committee on this bill, moved a clause to empower the Commissioners therein named to accept so much of any future loan* as they should have cash belonging to the public in their hands to pay for. This, he said, would obviate the great objection he had to the present bill, on account of its making the sinking-fund unalienable under any circumstances whatever; it would relieve that distress the country would otherwise be under, when, on account of a war, it might be necessary to raise a new loan: whenever that should be the case, his opinion was, that the minister should not only raise taxes sufficiently productive to pay the interest of the loan, but also sufficient to make good to the sinking fund whatsoever had been taken from it.

"If, therefore, for instance, at any future period a

---

* That is, to lend the Government any cash in their hands.

loan of six millions was proposed, and there was at that time one million in the hands of the Commissioners, in such case they should take a million of the loan, and the bonus or douceur thereupon should be received by them for the public. Thus Government would only have five millions to borrow instead of six; and from such a mode of proceeding, he said, it was evident great benefit would arise to the public."

Mr. Pitt's approval. "This clause was brought up by Mr. Fox, and received by Mr. Pitt with the strongest marks of approbation."

What objection? I defer a reply. At first sight, this clause of Mr. Fox's seems reasonable enough. The trustees for posterity, as they may be called, have money in their hands: the actual Government wants to borrow: what better customer can they find, than a Government that has always met its engagements? Besides; if they do not lend the money, they will buy stock with it; *i.e*, they will buy an annuity to be paid by the same Government; the Government therefore, is equally their customer in both cases; the form is different but not the substance. Was there then, any objection, hidden at the time and appearing afterwards? I defer answering this question till I have tried to illustrate the subject in my next chapter.*

Recapitulation. Such was Mr. Pitt's sinking-fund of 1786: which rejoiced the hearts of statesmen, patriots, and calculators, as giving promise of reducing the national debt at an expense which might easily be borne. A million annually, together with terminable annuities to fall in, would in 28 years accumulate a fund large enough to produce an annual revenue of 4 millions.

---

* See Chapter III. Section 7.

Peacenecessary. To be sure, peace was necessary for the purpose: and the long and tedious wars of the previous thirty years, had accustomed men to regard peace and war as almost equally natural; the seven years' war with France, and an equally long struggle with the colonies and their European supporters, having been nearly equal to the intervals of peace. Mr. Pitt however, might hope, that these contests had so far exhausted the present resources of the world, and the elements of strife, that a long repose might be anticipated: such a repose as Europe has actually enjoyed in the present century. Perhaps he counted on the pacifying effects of international communication, arising out of that commercial treaty of this very year, 1786, concluded with France, our ancient rival.

War followed. Twenty-eight years, from 1786, were to bring the sinking-fund up to such an amount as would produce four millions a year: these twenty-eight years extended to 1814, all but to the battle of Waterloo; through a period of unexampled European revolution, war, and expense. The National Debt grew from less than 250 millions to more than 800: the annual charge from less than ten millions to more than 31. Mr. Pitt hoped for peace and found war. If he had foreseen the future, he would not have talked about the accumulations of 28 years. Seven years after the establishment of his sinking-fund he was dragged into a war with France, accompanied in a short time by foreign subsidies, stoppage of the Bank of England, French revolutionary successes, and a war delirium in England.

Lord Grenville does not mention this. Have these unexpected events been sufficiently remembered in estimating this measure of 1786? It seems strange to me that Lord Grenville, who lived through them all, should not allude to them in accounting for the failure of the measure : perhaps this is explained by the fact that he had come to regard sinking-funds in themselves as delusions, and therefore sure to fail, under whatever circumstances.

VI.

1792 *another sinking-fund.* NO change of principle occurred during Mr. Pitt's lifetime ; but additions and alterations were made, as Dr. Hamilton tells us.*

" 1792.

" Another sinking-fund was established this year, of one per cent. on the nominal capital of each loan, to which the dividends on the capital redeemed by this fund, were to be added. When annuities for a longer term than forty-five years, or for lives were granted, the value which would remain after forty-five years, was appointed to be estimated, and one per cent. on that value set aside for their redemption. This fund was appointed to be kept separate, and applied for the redemption of the debts contracted subsequent to its institution, by which means it was estimated that every loan would be redeemed in forty-four years from its contraction.

" In the same year, £400,000 was granted in aid of the former sinking-fund, and £200,000 was granted by annual acts for the same purpose, till 1802, when the grant was rendered perpetual.

---
* Hamilton's " Inquiry," 1813, 99.

Savings by reduction of the rate of interest of the National Debt, were appointed to be added to that sinking-fund."

1784 *to* 1793 *diminution of debt.* This year, 1792, was the one before the new French war. We naturally inquire what reduction of debt had been effected. This was really considerable, being from 1786 to 1792 about six millions, or a million a year. A continuance of peace, accompanied by the rapidly growing resources of the country, might really have reduced the debt by one half in the period between 1786 and 1815.

1798 *deviation.* We cannot be surprised to find a change taking place in 1798. The year before had been one of the darkest in our financial history. Mr. McCulloch* says : " In 1797, the prospects of the country, owing to the successes of the French, the mutiny in the fleet, and other adverse circumstances, were by no means favourable ; and, in consequence, the price of 3 per cents. sunk, on the 20th of September, on the intelligence transpiring of an attempt to negotiate with the French republic having failed, *to* 47¾ being *the lowest price* to which they have *ever* fallen." Dr. Hamilton says as follows of 1798.

Hamilton's account : temporary suspension. " This year the application of one per cent. on the capital of the loans to the sinking-fund, was deviated from. A part of the loan (16 millions capital,) was charged on a tax then imposed, called the aid and contribution tax ; for which the income tax was substituted the following year. In like manner, a part, or the whole of the loans for several years, was charged on the income tax,† and no sinking-

---

* " Commercial Dictionary." 1840, 589.
† *i.e.*, the income tax was pledged to pay the interest.

fund of one per cent. provided for their redemption. The amount of capital for which no sinking-fund was provided, is £86,796,375. This system was abandoned in 1802, when all the loans were united, and the interests of these loans charged on the consolidated fund."

1798. Land tax redeemed. Even at this fearful period, Pitt did not forget his policy. As it was impossible to go on applying taxes to the reduction of debt, he adopted another scheme; that of capitalizing the land tax, and applying the proceeds to such reduction.

Hamilton's account. * "The present land tax commenced in 1692, when a valuation of the land was made, and although considerably below the real value at the time, it afforded a revenue of above £500,000, at one shilling per pound, including a like tax upon personal property, estimated at a very low rate. The valuation made at that time has never been altered; and the tax has been imposed annually till 1798, sometimes at one shilling, sometimes at two shillings, sometimes at three shillings, most frequently at four shillings, which rate it has never exceeded. . . . .

"In 1798 the land tax was rendered perpetual at four shillings per pound, and the proprietors were empowered to purchase the sums charged on their estates for capital in the three per cents. affording an equal dividend. If they did not accept this offer within a limited time, it might be sold to others for capital affording a dividend of one-fifth more than the tax purchased. The term for purchase has been since extended, and various regulations enacted, which it is unnecessary here to detail. In conse-

---

* Hamilton's "Inquiry." 1813, 105.

quence of these enactments, £23,941,057 capital in the three per cents. was transferred to the Commissioners for the Reduction of the National Debt, before 1st February, 1812, and £718,232 deducted from the dividends on the same."

VII.

Lord Colchester's diary. TWO entries in Lord Colchester's diary are worth noticing. In 1804,* " Feb. 1st, attended Board for Reduction of National Debt. The Sinking-fund supplies £1,500,000, to be laid out in the next quarter, and the capital stock redeemed is above £100,000,000."

Another entry of an earlier date, 7th June, 1799,† is less intelligible. " Supplies £31,000,000.—Ways and means, beyond the surplus of the Consolidated Fund, and Lottery, and Income Tax, a Loan of £15,500,000, whereof £11,000,000 to be charged upon the Income Tax, and £4,500,000 to be countervailed by the amount of the Sinking Fund, to redeem stock to the same amount."

Judging from the first entry, we may suppose that Lord Colchester believed the National Debt to have been lessened between 1786 and 1804, by the large sum of 100 millions, formed partly by the million a year appropriated in 1786; partly by terminable annuities that had fallen in; partly by the one per cent. set aside from a great part of the loans contracted; and finally by the compound interest on all these revenues. Hamilton is of opinion, that some reduction of debt was produced by these means, because

---

* Diary. 1. 478.   † Ib. 180—181.

as he thinks, the taxation of the country was really increased by them. The debt indeed between 1786 and 1804, was greatly increased by the war loans after 1793 : but it may still be true that it might have increased still faster in the absence of the Sinking-fund.

VIII.

1802. *Re-sumption of sinking-fund.* DURING the five years, from 1797 to 1802, national existence was at stake, and it was no time for ordinary sinking-funds. In 1802 came the peace, or armed truce, of Amiens. Pitt's influence renewed the practice of 1792.

"1802.

* " The two sinking-funds were united, applicable to the discharge of debts existing in 1802 ; and the system of a sinking-fund of one per cent. on loans subsequent to 1802, was revived, and has been followed in all the loans since,† except that of 1807, when Lord Henry Petty's system was adopted. The limitation of the sinking-fund to four millions,‡ enacted at its commencement, and a similar limitation in 1792, were repealed ; and the application of annuities whose term was expired, and of savings by the reduction of the rate of interest to the sinking-fund, was repealed."

---

* Hamilton, 1813, 101.   † Written in 1813.
‡ That is, to a principal producing an annual revenue of four millions.

IX.

1807. *New plan of Lord Henry Petty.*

AFTER the premature death of Pitt, and the formation of the Whig Ministry of All the Talents, an entirely new scheme was brought forward by the Chancellor of the Exchequer, Lord Henry Petty; the younger son of that Earl of Shelburne prominent in the time of Chatham and of Jeremy Bentham's youth. Lord Henry Petty lived to see all sinking-funds abolished and decried; and as the venerable Marquis of Lansdowne, witnessed other changes of higher importance.

"LORD HENRY PETTY'S SINKING-FUND.

Hamilton's account.

*" A new plan of finance was proposed to Parliament in 1807, by Lord Henry Petty, . . . and was adopted in the arrangement of the loan for that year.

" The annual expenditure during war, was estimated at 32 millions beyond what the surplus of the consolidated fund, and the annual taxes, could supply. The war taxes were estimated at 21 millions, viz., property tax $11\frac{1}{2}$ millions, and other articles, $9\frac{1}{2}$ millions. The annual deficiency to be supplied by loan was therefore 11 millions, which were proposed to be raised by mortgaging the war taxes to the extent of 10 per cent. on the sum borrowed; the surplus of which sum mortgaged, after paying for interest and management, was to form a sinking-fund for redeeming the debt, and thereby disengaging the part of the war taxes mortgaged in a certain

---

* Hamilton, 1813, 101.

number of years, according to the rate of interest at which the loan was contracted. Thus if the interest and management was 5 per cent. there would remain 5 per cent. as a sinking-fund, and this would pay off the debt in fourteen years. The sums proposed to be borrowed in this manner, were 12 millions for the first three years, 14 millions for the fourth, and 16 millions for each of the succeeding ten years, amounting altogether to 210 millions, for which, at the rate of 10 per cent. the whole of the war taxes would be mortgaged. But the debt contracted the first year being now paid off by the sinking-fund appropriated to it, the portion of the war taxes mortgaged for it would be set free, and be applicable to the loan of the following year; and another portion being set free the following and each succeeding year, these loans might be continued on this system without limitation of time."*

The apparent difficulty. I will not here enter on a detailed explanation of this scheme. It will probably occur to every reader, that the difficulty would consist in raising the required 10 per cent. interest: since in the 14th year, supposing the system to continue so long, 10 per cent. on 210 millions, would be 21 millions; and this large sum must have been raised by additional taxation.

Lord H. Petty's enthusiasm. This scheme well illustrates the hold which the sinking-fund had obtained on the minds of politicians. Enthusiasm was natural to Dr. Price and Mr. Pitt, the authors of the scheme of 1786: it was less to be expected in one of the Whig opposition, like Lord H. Petty. Yet he uttered the following remarks.†

---

* See also Lord Colchester's Diary. II. 91 note.
† Hamilton's " Inquiry." 1813, 194.

His speech. " To the consolidated fund the country has looked for the interest of its debt; and for its extinction, to the sinking-fund. The best eulogium that could be made on the sinking-fund, was the plain statement he had made. *There could be but one opinion in the House on the subject. It was owing to the institution of the sinking-fund that the country was not charged with a much larger amount of debt.* IT WAS AN ADVANTAGE GAINED BY NOTHING, and a system likely to be attended with still greater advantages. Therefore, independent of considerations of good faith, which should induce the House to hold and cling to a system once adopted, it was pledged to support it, having positive trial and experience of its utility."

Apology for. The most remarkable words are, " it was an advantage gained by nothing " : words that in the eyes of Lord Grenville and Mr. McCulloch, are I believe, utterly fallacious. Now to me it seems, that however much Lord Colchester and Lord Henry Petty and politicians generally overrated the actual results of Mr. Pitt's measure, there was a truth at the bottom of them, and there was a truth at the bottom of these enthusiastic words. I believe that under some circumstances a sinking fund might be so founded that advantages might be gained at no cost ; by which I understand that a sum of money might grow without expense to the ratepayers. The same principle justifies Dr. Price's assertion * that in the absence of a sinking fund a nation " obliges itself to return for every sum it borrows, infinitely greater sums."

Explanation. In my first chapter I explained this principle. I assumed that I became possessed

---

* Reversionary Payments 1783. 1. 181.

of an estate of £10,000 a year, burdened with a debt of £60,000. I showed that if I abstained from spending any of the income the first year, the £10,000 so saved would in about 14 years (at 5 per cent.) become £20,000; in about 28 years £40,000; and in far less than 42 years £60,000: whereas, if I began to abstain at the end of 28 or 30 years, I must give up many years' income to produce £60,000 by the same time. Now, if in the one case I sacrifice an expenditure of only 10 thousand, and in the other of 30 thousand, I may be said in the first case to make 20 thousand out of nothing.

It must be remembered that I suppose myself to sacrifice £10,000 of personal expenditure, and not of capital: because if it were capital, I should have made 5 per cent. or more of it; and at the conclusion of the 30 or 40 years I should be able with the results to pay off the 60,000 £.

Now the million levied for the sinking-fund in 1786, would have grown by another million early in the present century: and assuming that the first million was taken from the expenditure of the people, the additional million might be said to be "gained by nothing."

"Infinite" explained. Extending this illustration, Price's use of the word infinite is scarcely an exaggeration. For if in 1688, a million had been put into the hands of a commission, and had been invested at compound interest, the result now would be prodigious. Say that on the average it had doubled, not every fourteen years, but every twenty years. By the year 1888 the process would have gone on 200 years, and the million would have doubled ten times: it would therefore have grown into 1024 millions, or one-fourth more than our national debt. I assume that the million was at first

levied on the personal expenditure of the people : but even if it had been borrowed at 5 per cent., the 200 years' interest would have amounted to only ten millions; making altogether 11 millions. At an expense then, of 11 millions, there would have been created a principal nearly a hundred times as large. Another two hundred years would bring the one million to a sum that may almost be called infinite.

X.

1811. *Abbot.* IN the year 1811 we find Lord Colchester again recording the condition of the debt, and apparently believing that it was being, not reduced indeed, but greatly kept down.

"1811. **Wednesday, May 1st.* Went to the meeting of Commissioners for Reduction of the National Debt.

	Stock.
" Total Debt	£800,000,000.
" Whereof redeemed	200,000,000.
" Unredeemed	600,000,000.

" And for the current year thirteen millions sterling income to be applied to the redemption."

1812. *Hamilton.* This does not agree with the more precise account for the following year furnished by Hamilton ;† who makes all the amounts less than Lord Colchester ; and therefore the actual burden on the country less, though another year's war loans had been added.

Hamilton's figures are the following :

Amount of sinking-fund, 1st February, 1812, all but 12 millions
(or a million less than above)
Redeemed .... nearly 190 millions
(or 10 millions less than above)
Unredeemed .... less than 560 millions
(or 40 millions less than above)

---

* Lord Colchester, Diary II. 327.   † Hamilton's "Inquiry," 1813, 108.

1813. *Hamilton's work;* In 1813 appeared Hamilton's little volume, which has ever since been the authoritative work on the subject, and has deserved its reputation. It is short, pithy, " with few phrases and abundant facts"; resembling in this respect German rather than French workmanship;* but with all the numerous details so arranged as to bring out the conclusions intended. The third edition (1818), brings the accounts down to a later period.

not against sinking-funds. Hamilton, as I have already said, is falsely represented as an enemy to sinking-funds; and is falsely represented as having regarded Mr. Pitt's scheme as a failure. Hamilton really contended merely that Mr Pitt's scheme had not turned out the best possible : he held that the surplus income, when there was one, might have been used more advantageously. Far from condemning Mr. Pitt's sinking-fund, he maintained that it had caused increased taxation, and had thus kept the debt lower than it would have been. He calculated also that the debt would have been still less if the increased taxation had been used in the best possible way. Lord Grenville does not pretend that Hamilton agreed with him in condemning sinking-funds in general.

Decries Price's notions. Though however, Hamilton is not professedly an enemy to sinking-funds, he is but a lukewarm friend. He highly approves of efforts to reduce debt; he would support such a resolution as that of 1786, to apply a million £ a year to that purpose : but he sees no advantage in a formal system.† " In opposition to Dr. Price's

---

* For a comparison, written by a Frenchman, of German and French authorship, See *Revue des Deux Mondes.* 66, 1050. † Hamilton 1818, 182.

doctrine, it is maintained, that the separation of a sinking fund from the general revenue, is a measure of no efficacy whatever." I give elsewhere my reasons for believing that Hamilton is wrong, and that such separation is the most probable mode of securing accumulation at compound interest. The case is like the grant to Maynooth; which, so long as it appeared annually in the budget, was open to annual discussion. Under Mr. Pitt's scheme, the annual million, no doubt, might be objected to any year; but the sums already in the hands of the Commissioners, accumulated at compound interest without any annual appeal to Parliament. Both sinking fund and Maynooth might become subjects of discussion, but they would not *necessarily* be such every year.

XI.

1815 DURING the latter years of the war the pressure of taxation continued to be very severe; and as soon as peace was concluded, the income tax was rudely shaken off. Several years elapsed also, before the trade of the country resumed its natural level: there was great depression and difficulty.

1819 Even in 1819 there was much distress and dangerous political dissatisfaction. " War, our great customer, is dead," said Robert Owen. Yet another effort was made to reduce the debt: it was attempted to raise the revenue to an amount of 5 millions annually above the expenditure. But this proved too difficult.

1828—29, *end of direct sinking-fund.* Nine years afterwards appeared Lord Grenville's pamphlet, recanting the creed of his youth, and apologizing for the part he had taken in supporting Mr. Pitt's measure 42 years before. In the following year the statute of 10 Geo. IV abolished the old sinking-fund and established a new one, to consist of whatever surplus there might be of revenue over expenditure. This practice still prevails: a calculation is made quarterly, of the surplus of the previous four quarters; and one-fourth of this is applied to the purchase of government stocks, which to that extent are extinguished.

XII.

Since 1829, discouragement. SINCE the abolition in 1829 of the old sinking fund, discouragement has generally prevailed. The scheme of 1716 languished for 70 years, while the debt advanced: the scheme of 1786 shared the same fate; and the debt advanced still faster, until it reached an amount which a previous generation would have believed certain to crush any nation, however great and prosperous. In practice Dr. Price and Mr. Pitt had apparently failed: why should others hope to succeed?

Exceptions. Men indeed, were found, who could see below the surface; and who believed that in a time of peace we might do things which war made impossible. They thought that after the Napoleonic war had ceased, and the nation had recovered from the first pressure of the war burdens, new efforts ought to be made: especially they thought that the national prosperity which followed the free trade reforms of 1846, gave an admirable opportunity for a national effort.

Sir G. C. Lewis. Sir G. C. Lewis was one of these. Few statesmen have ever attained parliamentary influence so great as his, by means so honourable: by the force of a clear understanding, political knowledge, and unswerving integrity; without those showier qualities which are usually found necessary to the management of popular assemblies. To him it seemed that provision should be made to pay off debt contracted.

Plan of 1855. As Chancellor of the Exchequer in 1855, he found it necessary to provide for part of the expenses of the Crimean war, by contracting a loan for 16 millions.* He introduced " into the act sanctioning it, a clause providing for the gradual extinction of the debt by means of a sinking-fund."†

opposed. This clause " was not carried without serious opposition.‡ Mr. Disraeli, Mr. Gladstone, Mr. Cardwell, Mr. Labouchere, Mr. Henley, Mr. Ricardo, and other gentlemen of various shades of political opinion, resisted the proposal, on the ground that it was inconvenient and embarrassing to attempt to bind a future Parliament to a particular course in such a matter. Mr. Glyn, Mr. T. Baring, and other gentlemen of authority upon commercial questions, supported the Government, and the clause was carried on a division by a majority of 99. It was generally admitted that the clause could not be held so binding on a future Parliament as to preclude its repeal; but a great number of votes were recorded in its favour with a view ' to assert a principle'; the principle being, that the country should exert itself

---

* Northcote, Financial Policy. 1862, 267.   † *Ib.* 272.   ‡ *Ib.* 274.

in time of peace to pay off debts contracted in time of war. Mr. Gladstone, however, expressed his fear that many of those who intended to give their votes on this ground 'would be disposed to flinch from the maintenance of that principle, when they felt a strong pressure from without for the reduction of the hop, malt, insurance, or paper duties.'"

The plan explained: The plan was explained by Sir George Lewis in a subsequent budget speech.* " Before proceeding to the question of the taxation for the year, he added some particulars respecting the engagements into which Parliament had entered for the repayment of the debt contracted during the war. There were £7,000,000 of Exchequer-bonds to be redeemed by £2,000,000 a year; the last million would fall due in 1860. There was £250,000 to be paid by way of sinking-fund in 1857, and afterwards there was to be £1,500,000 a year to be paid, till the debt contracted during the war should be discharged."

afterwards swept away. Mr. Disraeli, who opposed the measure, had the satisfaction of cancelling it. The *Economist*† says :—" There is a most unpopular sort of finance, to which, notwithstanding its unpopularity, some attention should be paid. We have within the last few years augmented our debt materially. . . . . The reason is that we have made little effort to repay the loans which were made during the Crimean war. Several Exchequer-bonds which were to be paid 'like a bill of exchange,' are still unpaid, although the time at which they first fell due is long past. The sinking-fund which Sir G. Lewis proposed to maintain out of the surplus revenue was swept away by Mr. Disraeli with the consent of Parliament.

---

* *Ib.* 307.   † *Economist,* 11 April, 1863, 395, col. 2.

Impossible to revive it. "It would be childish to propose to revive a great scheme for acting upon our debt after such a failure as the last. Sir G. Lewis's sinking-fund was announced when he raised a loan, it might almost be said to be a condition of that loan; in the case of a weak state without credit it *would* be so said; it was sanctioned by an express resolution of Parliament; it was framed on the best principle; we borrowed in the stock in which most money could be raised most cheaply; we were to employ our actual surplus revenue to a moderate extent in the purchase of the cheapest stock which we could buy. Yet even this sinking-fund was abolished at once with general approbation. No one can now, therefore, hope for greater success in a similar undertaking, for he cannot hope for even equal advantages."

XIII.

Terminable annuities. SINCE then, Parliament cannot bind itself for the future, and since public opinion does not relish the maintenance of an open and avowed sinking fund, the only remaining modes of reducing our debt are, first, the precarious one of securing in the Budget an annual surplus; and secondly, the selling of terminable annuities. Parliament and public opinion, will secure the fulfilment of any bargain once made with individuals or bodies corporate, for annuities long or short, favourable or adverse.

Life annuities. The sale of life annuities goes on regularly. The sum annually paid as interest on the national debt and for expenses of management, is about 26 millions; but if the whole debt were in the form of 3 per cents, the annual payment would be about a million and a quarter less: this million and a quarter is a sinking fund, in the form of terminable annuities. A man who has no heirs, or none he values, and who wants to secure a certain income for the remainder of his life, hands over his principal to the Government, and is promised 5 or 6 or 7 per cent., according to his age. The Government pays a high rate for a short time, instead of 3 per cent. for ever. The *Economist* * says:—"We now sell life annuities, and apply the proceeds to the reduction of the debt. This amount is at present very small; but there is no reason why it should not be increased. By offering better terms for the sale of life annuities than other people, we might sell any quantity of them which we liked. The process entails a certain increase of annual charge, but not a very great increase if the annuities created are long annuities; and it has the advantage of being the sole scheme by which our debt can ever be liquidated without calling upon Parliament at once for a large sum of money, which hardly any Government will like to ask for, and hardly any popular Assembly will ever grant."

Whether there is an indefinitely large demand for life annuities, whether the terms the Government would have to concede would be very unfavourable, whether it is desirable to encourage men to sink their principal and thus disappoint their natural heirs, are questions I do not here discuss.

Other terminable annuities. But we have frequently borrowed on other terminable annuities: we have recently experienced the pleasure of seeing

---

* *Economist*, 11 April, 1863. 395 col. 2.

a large diminution in the annual charge for debt, when certain terminable annuities ceased. It is alleged however, that this forms a very improvident arrangement; and that the unfortunate and unfair provisions of Sir Robert Peel's income tax bill, which by taxing the gross amount of these annuities, confiscated part of the principal, have rendered it impossible at present to make reasonable terms.

<small>1860, Mr. Hubbard's objections: rate of Consols.</small> On the 27th July, 1860, Mr. Hubbard called the attention of the House to the proposal of the Government, to create terminable annuities, sufficient to raise several millions for the purpose of fortifications.*

" Mr. Hubbard would . . . . put before the House the usual means by which public loans were raised in this country. He would first say a few words on loans raised in the shape of Consolidated three per cents.: no less a sum than £16,000,000 had thus been raised in 1855. The price of that loan was 88 per cent., and the discount to the contractor for his risk, 2 per cent., which he agreed was a fair allowance. The country therefore had the opportunity of raising money at £3. 8s. per cent.

" The next instance was that of the following year, when a loan of £5,000,000 was contracted for at £90.; the interest to the contractor was 6s. 6d., making the price of stock to him £89. 13s. 6d. The market price was £91.; therefore the contractor had an advantage over the public of only £1. 6s. 6d. .

. . . .

" It thus appeared that money could be raised on Consols, and repaid without disturbing the market, and that the money could be obtained by Govern-

---

* Statistical Journal. Sept. 1860. 398.

ment at about 2 per cent. only above the regular market price; and although it was true that the funds were generally high when the Government broker sold out, and low when he bought in, that was not peculiar to the case of raising money by means of stock, but applied to all descriptions of loan. Allowing 2 per cent. to be lost in the first instance in the turn of the market, and assuming that 2 per cent. more would be lost before they could replace it through the medium of the Commissioners for the Reduction of the National Debt, that would be 4 per cent. spread over thirty years, or about $\frac{1}{4}$ per cent., which would amount to £3. 12s. 6d., as the entire cost of raising public money through Consols.

Rate of Terminable Annuities: Income Tax. "He now came to the question of raising money by Terminable Annuities; and he would allude to the one mentioned the other day by the First Lord of the Treasury, and which he termed the dead-weight annuity. The sum of £585,745 was taken by the Bank in 1823, at a time when the funds were exceedingly disturbed, so that they could only make an approximation, not only of the value at which it would be in Consols, but the rate of interest which the Bank of England derived from the investment. They yielded an interest of £4. 2s. 1d. In 1842, when the income tax was imposed through the medium of an old Act of Parliament, it made a grievous mistake, for it taxed both capital and interest, and instead of receiving £4. 2s. 1d., the Bank was obliged to recast the whole schedule, and reduce the interest to £3. 18s. 2d. In April, 1847, there was a further change in the income tax, which forced them again to recast their schedule, and the interest was reduced to £3. 15s. 6d.; and in 1851 it was again reduced to £3. 5s. 7d., and in October of the same year to £3. 1s 9d. So that they *might well imagine how uncertain a security this was, and how little capitalists could look forward to it as a valid security.*"

Superiority of Consols, Desirable as it may be for the Government to borrow in terminable annuities, as being the only mode of binding Parliament to a resolution in favour of reducing the debt, I fear we must concede that the sacrifice is too great. The injustice committed by Sir Robert Peel, and repeated by subsequent ministers, has helped to deprive us of this resource. But the disadvantage of borrowing on terminable annuities does not arise from this incident alone. The superiority of Consols as a Government Stock has been shown by Mr. Newmarch.*

shown by Mr. Newmarch. " Whether for good or evil ends, but certainly on the whole for good ends, the Stock Exchange is a vast market where men employ masses of capital in dealing backwards and forwards in the different Stocks ; and, like all other great markets, custom, convenience, and self-interest have gradually set up certain conditions which govern in a great measure the movements of the whole body of operators. One of the best established of these conditions is, that any new kind of Stock, attempted to be introduced with success, must be *marketable* at all times and to any extent, it must be of a nature which everybody understands —it must be free from new conditions—and it must be also free from future contingencies in the estimation of which hardly two persons will agree. Now, it is the fact, that for the last hundred years the 3 per cent. Consols have been the kind of fund

---

* Statistical Journal. "Loans raised by Mr. Pitt." 18. 130.

which, beyond all others, has fulfilled these conditions of eligibility in the most pre-eminent degree From the circumstance of the amount of the funded capital of this Stock always greatly exceeding in magnitude the funded capital of any other kind of Stock, Consols have admitted of speculative operations being carried on in them far beyond anything that could be prudently undertaken in any other fund ; and hence it has followed, that from the nature, and habit, and constitution of the Stock Market, 3 per cent. Consols have relatively been worth more to the dealers in that market than any other kind of Stock ; and the higher relative price so existing, however ridiculous it may appear to abstract reasoners, is a price perfectly legitimate on all grounds of dealing. And one of the main reasons of the preference of Consols, after allowing for the magnitude of the fund, *has always been their exemption from embarrassing hazards of future redemption—* particularly as they have the great safeguard of a year's notice being necessary before the holders can be compelled to accept payment at par."

XIV.

What remains ? IT seems therefore, that with or without the injustice inflicted by the income-tax, the borrowing on terminable annuities must cost more than the borrowing on Consols. What remains then ? The nation will not pay off debt with its eyes open : to blind it by terminable annuities is too expensive.

1866, 1867.   An ingenious scheme has been pro-
Mr. Gladstone pounded. Who was the author of it I

and Mr. Disraeli. have not heard. The public knows only that Mr. Gladstone brought it forward in 1866, and that Mr. Disraeli adopted it in 1867. I have shown that both these statesmen opposed Sir G. C. Lewis's measure in 1855: but it must be remembered that Mr. Gladstone's objections were to the possibility, not to the desirableness, of such a sinking-fund. You may snatch a vote in its favour, but you cannot bind future Parliaments: you will find that demands for remission of taxation will crush your measure. Mr. Gladstone's prophecy turned out to be a true one: the bills on futurity were dishonoured.

Their scheme. Mr. Gladstone's measure of 1866 will be found fully explained by the *Economist*.*

"The State undertook, many years since, to be the bankers of the poorer classes, and indeed, if the matter is looked to, the Chancellor of the Exchequer is the largest deposit banker, and by far the largest fundholder, in the nation. These poor people's— these savings' banks—moneys were invested in Stocks at high prices, and would, if repaid, have to be repaid by sales at low prices. The same cause which occasioned the withdrawal would occasion also the reduction of the price. Accordingly, a very great loss was incurred. Some years ago, not with a view of lessening the loss, which no book-keeping could alter, but of making the account look clearer, Mr. Gladstone cancelled Stock bought with £24,000,000 of savings' bank money, and turned it into a large I O U, a book debt of the nation. Of course, as between the depositors and the State, this operation had no effect; we must pay the money we received: it is a transfer from one head of the

---

* *Economist*, May 5, 1866. 527, col. 1.

national ledger to another, and no more. But upon that £24,000,000 of debt so created Mr. Gladstone has great facilities for acting,—he is both debtor and creditor. He took certain poor persons' moneys and bought Stock with them. If he, with the aid of Parliament, choose to turn that Stock into any other sort of annuity there is no one to hinder him or to question what he does. In fact, he proposes to turn this £24,000,000 of book debt into annuities ending in 1885. This would cost annually one million sterling. At present the charge of the £24,000,000 debt is £720,000; afterwards it will be £1,725,000."

Discreditable to the nation. For the remainder of the scheme I must refer to the *Economist*. Mr. Gladstone told Sir G. C. Lewis, that the nation would not consent to pay its debt openly: he believed that the nation would consent to pay it when it appeared in the form of annuities. Probably he was right: but the fact was discreditable to the financial opinions of the public. It is a bad state of affairs when the world has to be treated like a peevish child. The course taken by Sir G. C. Lewis was philosophical and honest: that taken by Mr. Gladstone was politic, and perhaps statesmanlike.

Equivalent to Mr. Pitt's sinking fund. This annuity scheme is really Mr. Pitt's sinking fund of 1786, on a small scale, and ingeniously disguised. Mr. Pitt proposed to take a million a year from the proceeds of the taxes, to invest this million in the hands of Commissioners, and to instruct them to increase this fund by interest and compound interest. If the rate of interest they could get should turn out to be 5 per cent., they would accumulate in about 14 years, no less than 20 millions; and in 16 years, 24 millions. Mr. Gladstone also proposed to take a million a year from the proceeds of taxation, and under the form of annuities terminable in 1885, to accumulate a fund at compound interest: he calculated that in 1885, at the present low rate of interest, the fund would amount to 24 millions. Interest at 5 per cent. would produce 24 millions in 16 years: the present low rate would require 19 years to produce that sum. This difference of 3 years may appear small; but it is not so. In the one case the million is paid for 16 years, in the other for 19: in the one case the interest amounts to 8 millions, in the other to only 5.

	Payments from taxation.	Compound Interest.	Total.
When interest is at 5 per cent.	16 millions	8 millions	24 millions
At present low rate of interest	19 ,,	5 ,,	24 ,,

In the one case the interest is half as much as the principal: in the other case it is little more than a fourth.

Why the Economist did not put it in this light. The *Economist* was pleased to avoid this direct explanation: doubtless the editor was restrained by patriotic motives: he might well fear that if the opposition got hold of the clear notion that the scheme was the old sinking fund in disguise, they would turn it out of doors. Wrapped up in the form of terminable annuities, and safe from Mr. Hubbard's exposition of the loss attending terminable annuities generally, it might escape detection and denunciation.

Mr. Disraeli adopted the measure. The change of ministry put an end to the proposal. Happily, Mr. Disraeli on succeeding to Mr. Gladstone's office, adopted this measure: a proceeding highly creditable to his candour.

XV.

Recapitulation. I HAVE thus given an account of the principal sinking funds, beginning with that of 1716 and ending with that of 150 years later.

1716. After the great accumulation of debt caused by the War of the Succession, and closed by the Peace of Utrecht, Sir Robert Walpole established the first sinking fund : it was to consist of the surplus of the *South Sea, Aggregate,* and *General Funds,* together with the savings caused by the reduction in the rate of interest. The fund was maintained even when fresh loans were made. It " continued nominally in the accounts of the exchequer during 70 years."

1786. After the conclusion of the American War, " the various branches of revenue existing, were united under the name of the consolidated fund. One million was ordered to be handed over annually to Commissioners, who were instructed to apply it to the accumulation of a fund at compound interest."

1792. " Another sinking fund was established this year," consisting principally of " one per cent. on the nominal capital of each loan."

1798. The political and financial distress of the country, compelled the abandonment of this one per cent. on loans.

1802. On the conclusion of the Peace of Amiens, the one per cent. on loans was revived, and was generally continued during the resumed war.

1807. After the death of Mr. Pitt, Lord Henry Petty as Chancellor of the Exchequer, introduced a new scheme, which continued only one year, being dropped by his successors.

1819. For many years after the conclusion of peace in 1815, there was great distress and political discontent. Yet in 1819 an effort was made to raise 5 millions a year surplus taxation, to discharge part of the debt. As a matter of course, the measure failed.

1829. Ten years later, Mr. Pitt's sinking fund was abolished. The long continued war had rendered the scheme impossible : such a peace as that beginning with 1815, might have shown a different result.

1855. These failures have made the term sinking fund almost one of reproach. Yet in 1855, Sir G. C. Lewis made another effort to provide for the repayment of new war loans. He was opposed, but carried his measure : which however, was subsequently annulled.

1860. Five years later, Mr. Gladstone proposed to raise money for fortifications, by the sale of terminable annuities, (not for lives). Mr. Hubbard showed that this mode of raising money was a very expensive one, and that the 3 per cent. Consols constituted the true resource for borrowing.

1866—67. In 1866 Mr. Gladstone propounded an ingenious plan for dealing with the deposits in savings' banks. The 24 millions in the hands of Government were to be turned into annuities expiring in 1885. A million a year of additional taxation would be necessary for the purpose. Happily, Mr. Disraeli has adopted the scheme. Virtually, it is nothing more than Mr. Pitt's scheme, taken from Dr. Price, of setting aside a million a year, to accumulate at compound interest.

CHAPTER III.

ILLUSTRATION AND EXPLANATIONS.

I.

PART I.

Explanations required in last chapter. IN the last chapter I gave a sketch of the different British sinking funds. But I purposely delayed an investigation of certain difficulties which presented themselves: I did not inquire what was the effect of Mr. Fox's clause in 1786; nor what truth there was in Dr. Price's assertion, that a nation might advantageously borrow at simple interest and at the same time accumulate at compound interest; nor how far it is desirable to go on with the sinking fund in time of war, when fresh loans are contracted.

I now offer an illustration. In the present chapter I will try to supply these omissions. To accomplish this I will imagine a sinking fund conducted quite differently from those I have recorded. I will do this at some length; not because I regard this scheme as feasible; but because by working it out into many particulars, I hope to make it more useful as an illustration, and to impress it more fully upon the mind.

Source of the difficulties to be explained. Our past sinking funds have proceeded by applying surplus taxation to the purchase of Government stocks. The Commissioners have bought stock in the market, and have had it transferred to themselves. This is the first difficulty with most readers. If the Government, having previously borrowed 10 millions in one year, had raised a surplus in each of the next ten years, and in each of those ten years had repaid one million, that course would have been intelligible to all; but it is not so well understood that the purchase of stock is a discharge of debt. Then again there is the interest on these purchases : the Government raises as before taxes to pay interest on the stocks now standing in the names of the Commissioners; this interest is handed over to the Commissioners, who use it in the purchase of further stocks. It is felt all the time that the Commission is a limb of the Government; that the Government is in fact paying interest to itself; and so the whole thing looks like a mere matter of account, if not something like a juggle.

II.

Suppose savings applied to India; THIS difficulty would be removed if the government, instead of buying stock, actually paid off debt which it owed. But it would also be removed, if the Government deposited its savings somewhere, just as a private person deposits his savings with a banker. Let us suppose then, that it is determined to use India as the Government banker. That vast crown possession wants railroads, tanks, canals : let the national savings be applied to constructing these works.

as an utopian scheme, I must beg to be understood as suggesting this purely as an utopian scheme. I am quite aware that it would not be tolerated by the nation or by Parliament, that we should make an immense investment of savings in a distant country, which may improve so much as to become capable of self-government, and from which therefore, we may have to retire; a country too, already an object of envy to our European neighbours, and which would become a still richer prize by continued outlay.

by loan to Indian Government. Imagine however, that each million saved is transmitted to India, as a loan to its Government; which is responsible for its safe application, and for the payment of 5 per cent. interest. Many millions have actually been lent by private persons to the Indian Government, for the construction of railways; the remuneration being interest at 5 per cent. and a possible share of profits; and with such success that several of the lines are paying rather more than the 5 per cent.

Dr. Price's principle. To satisfy Dr. Price and Mr. Pitt, the interest on this million should not be sent home, but should be also invested at 5 per cent., and in the third year and in all succeeding years, the augmented interest should also be invested. In short the investment should be made in India at 5 per cent. compound interest.

A million each year. Mr. Pitt's scheme in 1786 provided for an annual payment of a million from the taxes. Say that we now raised such a surplus, and remitted a million every year to India, during fourteen years. At the end of this period, supposing the Indian Government paid all the expenses of management, our accumulated investment would be about 20 millions. If the process were continued, the 20 millions would become 40 in about another fourteen years; and if during those fourteen years the annual million were also still sent, our whole investment in 28 years would be about 60 millions. Continuing in the same way, the investment at the end of 84 years would be 1,260 millions ; or half as much again as our national debt.

III.

Possibility : THIS is not a mere trick of figures, but a result physically possible. The Indian railways have to a great extent been formed with capital borrowed at 5 per cent. and some contingent profit. It is true that the railways have been constructed, as in England, by joint stock companies : but there is this difference between India and England, that here the companies incur all the risk, there it is not so. The Indian Government, in order to secure the immediate construction of the lines, have guaranteed 5 per cent. dividend to the shareholders. The English shareholders therefore, have the security of the Indian Government. But that Government is indifferent as to whose money it is that they guarantee : if a million a year were remitted for these purposes by the British Government, that would as a matter of course, come under the guarantee.

amounts : If this scheme had been begun about
railways ; 14 years ago, the investment, with compound interest similarly laid out, would now be 20 millions. This may seem a large sum : yet what is it in such a country ? In England the capital of the railways is reckoned by hundreds of millions : though the Indian cost per mile is far less, the country is vastly greater : I have mentioned that already the

earnings of some of the lines exceed the guaranteed 5 per cent.; there is hope therefore, that a great extension of railways will be possible. Twenty millions, the fourteen years' accumulation, might be multiplied many times, before this mode of investment was exhausted.

water. Many other kinds of permanent improvements are wanted: especially, the means of storing and distributing water. At present, continued drought brings with it consequences, such as it sickens one to read of. The Irish famine of twenty years ago was horrible : it was caused by an unexampled failure of the potato : it was not preventible, unless by a previous prohibition of growing potatoes as the main food of the people ; an interference not sanctioned by our prevalent notions of the functions of Government. What if the Irish famine had been preventible ? What if the due distribution of water was all that was wanted ? Should we not have been laying out money ever since, in building tanks and constructing canals? Now in India, famines are constantly occurring : it is stated that there have been three in twelve years. The scale of misery is gigantic : in the one province of Orissa,* it is believed that the late famine destroyed one-fifth of the population ; just as if four millions had died in England, or a million and a half in Ireland twenty years ago, or 600,000 in London. The actual deaths in Orissa are estimated at 750,000 or perhaps a million. To mitigate such calamities, the old conquerors of India did in fact construct vast tanks and watercourses : all these want restoring. Here there is room for great investments, for which the Indian Government might well borrow money at 5 per cent.,

---
* *Spectator*, 1996. 1077. There must be a good deal of conjecture in these statements; and conjectural statistics are particularly unsatisfactory.

even if some of the interest had to be paid out of taxation.

Investments generally. But we need not fear that profitable investments would be wanting. Capital hitherto, has been scarce in India, as it always is in countries where for centuries there has been no security. That this security is still imperfect even in our possessions, is I fear true: that it is still more defective in native states is indisputable. An interesting paper attributed to a native, though written in English,* praises the administration of criminal justice, but only apologizes for the absence of civil justice. Violence is repressed; chicanery flourishes. *Though want of security: native states.* "In cities and towns, in the midst of squares and bazaars, the banker sits with the same ease and contentment of mind with his iron chest loaded with gold and silver coins, and his writing-box containing cheques, notes, drafts, and hundis, as he would do in the British cities of Delhi and Agra. The confectioner has the same flourishing and attractive shop as his brethren in Benares and Allahabad, and the artizan produces the same fancy articles as the members of his craft in other parts of the country. The carpenter works with his chisel with the same independence of spirit as his race throughout India; and the blacksmith beats his anvil and sings his ballad in a mood of mind equally expressive of happiness and contentment. In a word, security of life and property in a native state is not less than it is in the British districts, and forced labour is to the full as restricted in the one as in the other."

On the other hand:—" There are officers to decide on civil suits, who, the civil law being in essentials

---

* *Spectator*, April 27. 1867. 462—464.

divine, ought to be priests, but who in practice are the nominees and favourites of the local authorities, without learning, or honour, or influence. Except in matters of marriage, inheritance, or divorce, where the law is too dear for them and people are apt to use their swords, they sell their decisions, and the consequent insecurity of all property, except land, is incomparably the greatest evil in a Native State. The only remedy is an appeal to the Prince, who is often a nullity, or to the plaintiff who can be influenced in different ways, through his relations, or his women, or his children, or his friends, or something or somebody wholly apart from justice. Civil justice, as we understand it, scarcely exists."

Without security there will be little accumulation: therefore, till the habits of the people and the modes of administration are greatly altered, capital will be scarce; the rate of interest will be high; and there will be abundance of room for the investment of British funds.

IV.

Comparison of Great Britain and India. IF we recollect the aggregate value of English property, we shall the more readily believe that it will be long before India is saturated with capital. By means of the probate of wills and the tax on successions to realty, we know pretty nearly what Englishmen really possess. It is believed that the whole property of the British Isles is not less than six thousand millions. The population of our Indian possessions is nearly five times as great as ours; and without assuming the possibility of bringing up Indian property to thirty thousand millions, we may conjecture that it might be possible to gradually invest 20 or 100 or 1,000 millions, without any alarming results.

Must be done gradually, I have assumed that these investments are made gradually, beginning with only one million the first year : also that the operation having begun 14 years ago, there would now be 20 millions invested. In fact, without allowing for the Great Ganges Canal, or other means of distributing water, the railroads alone would have been far more than sufficient to swallow up the 20 millions, and would have well paid 5 per cent. Next year the supply of capital would be two millions: viz., the million sent over, and the interest on the 20 millions accumulated.

for want of labourers; If an attempt were made to invest a large sum at once, great difficulties would occur : for at the present moment, as we are told, a want of labourers is felt; and to such a degree, as not only to have greatly raised the scale of wages, but even to make any large extension of outlay on public works impossible.

but steady progress would secure these. No doubt, in this, as in other productive operations, a steady demand would secure a supply. Immigrants would be found : not indeed Europeans, whose bringing up in a temperate climate unfits them for a burning Asiatic sun : but Chinese or other Eastern races, who show themselves ready to go where employment, wages, and security, are to be enjoyed. When it came to be understood through the East, that the Indian Government systematically executed public works, and each year in an increasing ratio; and that therefore, every year, more and more labourers were employed; immigration would supply all that was wanted.

Increased amounts hereafter. It may be objected that this would be quite conceivable, so long as the annual outlay was a million, or even five millions: but that the scheme supposes a continuance of the process of accumulation, until the invested fund amounted to 1,200 millions, and the annual interest to 60 millions: how could such an amount be used? I reply that I am not making any pretensions to political prophecy: I should as soon think of foretelling the weather for 84 years. I do not predict that India will be an English possession in the next century; nor that, if it is an English possession, it will be capable of absorbing each year fifty or sixty millions in public investments. It will however, diminish the apparent absurdity, to recollect that the aggregate annual savings of England, with a fifth of the Indian population, are computed at more than twice this sum.*

Australia may be added. But India is not our only possession. To say nothing of Canada, a precarious dependency, there is Australia, whose population is now as large as that of our American Colonies when they seceded, and we thought ourselves ruined by the loss. What may be the population of Australia eighty-four years hence? Just that period has elapsed since we acknowledged the United States independent: their numbers have multiplied tenfold: in a period of the same length the Australians may become as numerous as the Americans are now. Emigration is more difficult, no doubt: but the means of transport are facilitated; the habit of moving from place to place has been formed; and people now shrink less from a voyage to the Antipodes, than they did fifty years ago from crossing

---

* *Economist*, 12th and 19th Dec., 1863, reckons them at 130 millions.

the Atlantic. Australia therefore, might be added
to India as a field for investment; and judging from
past experience, a continent containing hereafter
thirty millions of European descent, and principally
of English descent, with unoccupied land of indefinite
area, would easily absorb vast capitals annually at
an interest of 5 per cent.

V.

A new colonial system might follow. AN enthusiast might regard this system as a new era in colonization:
he might contend that it was a means of
binding colonies to the mother country with a golden
chain. New countries greatly want capital: and if
this were supplied, so far as public purposes are
concerned, and at a moderate rate such as 5 per
cent., there would be a strong motive on the colonial
side for continued dependence. We have ceased to
use the colony as a protected market; we are withdrawing from its military and naval defence; and
continued connection with us is precarious; but if
we became the patron in money matters, supplying
capital, and taking only a moderate share of the
gains, the old attachment might revive.

VI.

Explanations: suppose Indian investment 1786. LET us now go back to 1786, and
compare the scheme of that year
with my imaginary one: let us imagine
that Pitt had combined his measure with

his Indian bill passed not many years before; and had proposed, subject to the approbation of his Board of Control, that the East India Company should receive a million a year from England, should lay it out in tanks and watercourses and other productive works; paying 5 per cent. interest, and again investing this interest in the same way. The investments would have been, in 1786-7, 1 million; 1787-8, 2,050,000; 1800-1, 20 millions (about).

The actual course. The course really pursued was different. In the first year the Sinking Fund Commissioners laid out a million in buying Consols,* just as the Bank of England might have done: the Consols so purchased were transferred to the Commissioners, just as they would have been to the Bank of England. In the second year, the Commissioners laid out a second million in buying Consols, which were also transferred to them; but in this second year, there was interest coming in on the first year's purchase; this interest was likewise laid out in buying Consols. Therefore at the end of the second year the Commissioners held Consols which had cost them more than 2 millions.

Comparison: similarity; In both cases the Commissioners would have laid out their money and received security. In the Indian scheme they would have had the security of the Indian Government and of the productive works executed: and in the other scheme they had the security of the British Government. In both schemes too, the interest received would have been invested in the same security as the original principal.

dissimilarity: But there is one remarkable difference in the two modes. In the Indian case, a sum of

---

* I say Consols for shortness though I do not mean to say that the Commissioners were forbidden to buy other Government Stocks.

money would have been lent in each of the years, and 5 per cent. covenanted to be paid. In the actual case, the rate of interest would be different for each year. It is true that Consols always pay 3 per cent. : and if the Commissioners bought at par, they would get just 3 per cent. : but the Commissioners, like the Bank, or any other buyer, must purchase at the price of the day ; and this price is very variable. In 10 or 12 years before 1792, the 3 per cents. varied from 54 to 96 : that is the rate of interest to be obtained was nearly 6 per cent. at one time and little more than 3 per cent. at another. Under the Indian scheme then, the rate of interest would have been uniformly 5 per cent. : under the actual scheme it was very variable.

an actual evil in rates of interest. And this illustration exhibits a serious disadvantage of the English sinking-funds. They made their investments in a variable security ; and unfortunately, made them for the most part when that security was high, and the interest to be obtained was low. The very fact of their investing raised the price of the funds, not merely by taking a quantity from the market, but also by improving the credit of the Government. In 1716, no doubt, this was the very aim proposed : Sir Robert Walpole had to strive first of all to strengthen the new dynasty, and he might well, in the presence of such a duty, leave posterity to deal with the debt. In 1786 however, Pitt really wanted to lessen the debt ; and as he was bent on peace, and hoped for peace, he did not expect to be a borrower, and had no special reason for wishing to see the funds high. To employ his million a year therefore, in buying Consols, was to be constantly reducing the rate of interest which his sinking-fund would get.

VII.

Mr. Fox's clause: LET us now look at the clause introduced by Mr. Fox into the bill of 1786. This clause was "to empower the Commissioners to accept so much of any future loan as they should have cash belonging to the public in their hands to pay for." But "whenever that should be the case, his opinion was, that the minister should not only raise taxes sufficiently productive to pay the interest of the loan, but also sufficient to make good to the sinking-fund whatsoever had been taken from it."

tried by the Indian case. How would this have worked if the sinking fund had gone to India? War broke out in 1793, and we soon had to borrow. Suppose that in 1794, Mr. Pitt was about to remit his quarterly amount of 250,000 £.: that instead of doing this he used the sum for the army, and promised that on the return of peace it should be replaced. This is what the Commissioners would do under Mr. Fox's clause: they would take part of the loan; that is, they would leave the money in Mr. Pitt's hands, and would receive Consols for it, at the market price: Consols being a promise to pay, not indeed any capital sum, but a perpetual annuity.

Of course in the Indian case, the principal, being all invested in permanent improvements, could not be realized and brought back to England: but neither did Mr. Fox propose that the Commissioners should realize their principal, by selling part of their stocks: it was only cash in hand, uninvested, that he would touch.

What objection? Is there any objection to the provision introduced by Mr. Fox and approved by Mr. Pitt?

The Government wants money, and has to borrow; the Commissioners have money in hand; or taking the Indian case, the Government has money which it is about to remit: is not it expedient that the Government should use this money, with the understanding that on the return of peace, taxes should be levied to replace it?

The course generally unintelligible. Financially, I fear, it is impossible to defend the continuing the operations of the sinking fund in a time of war and loans: Hamilton has, no doubt, shown that a serious loss was caused by attempting it; not that he condemns the sinking fund on the whole, because he concedes that it caused increased taxation and a real diminution of debt: he only contends that with the same taxation the debt might have been diminished still further in the absence of the expensive apparatus of Commissioners and their nominal redemption.

One objection seems to me to be the same here as in the other parts of the scheme; that the public could not understand what was going on. If the sum of a million a year had been really remitted to India for investment, that would have been understood; and so would have been the fact that in about fourteen years, this with compound interest would amount to 20 millions. If also, under such a system a war loan had been wanted; and Mr. Pitt had said, I will keep back my remittances to India till time of peace, and then I will raise additional taxation, and will pay to India all I have kept back, together with compound interest; this course would have been easily intelligible. When peace arrived, the nation would have cried out for an effort to fulfil the intention of bringing up the arrears.

Public opinion the only safe guardian. The complexity of the scheme of 1786 seems to me fatal: the only chance, I imagine, of permanently carrying out any measure for repayment of debt, would be to put it under the guardianship of public opinion; and public opinion cannot act unless the public clearly understands what is being done. I do not mean that this would be a reason for adopting a scheme such as this utopian one of mine, which I have advanced merely for illustration: but I do mean that some scheme should be sought such as the world at large might appreciate and watch over.

VIII.

Dr. Price's objection; DR. PRICE indeed, condemned the taking the Commissioners' cash, even in times of loans. He says* that the fund has been generally alienated. "In order to justify this, it has been usual to plead, that when money is wanted, it makes no difference, whether it is taken from hence, or procured by making a new loan. But in truth the difference between these two methods of procuring money is no less than *infinite*. For by employing the SINKING - FUND in bearing current expenses, rather than borrowing *new* money on new funds; the State, in order to avoid giving *simple interest* for money, is made to alienate money that *must* have otherwise been improved at *compound interest*; and which in time would have *necessarily* increased to *any* sum."

Illustrated. Let us look at this by the light of my Indian scheme. Mr. Pitt finds in a particular year, that his revenue just equals his necessary expenditure; and that if he remits the stipulated million to

---
* "Reversionary Payments." 1783. I. 209.

India, he will have to borrow the same sum. Ought he to remit and borrow ; or ought he to keep back the million ? Remit and borrow, says Price : keep back the million, says Hamilton.

Dr. Price's reasons. Dr. Price says, if the million is remitted it will produce £50,000 the first year, £52,500 the second year, and by the end of 14 years will become two millions ; by the end of 100 years, 128 millions. But the million borrowed will not increase in this way, nor increase at all : simply, £50,000 a year will be paid for interest. At the end of 100 years, the whole interest paid will amount to five millions, whereas, the addition to the Indian million will be 127 millions. This is what Lord Henry Petty called making 122 millions out of nothing.

He supposes the £50,000 to be taxes paid out of personal expenditure. Now, if the annual £50,000 of interest, as I have remarked before, were taken from the personal expenditure of the country, the nation would lose only the gratification which the £50,000 a year would purchase : but if it were taken from the capital of the country, the nation would lose not only the million but the profits on it, and possibly second profits on the first profits capitalized. I think, however, we may fairly regard taxes generally as paid out of personal expenditure, and not out of capital.

Hamilton's reasons ; continued war. But Hamilton raised an objection of a different kind. It was during years of continued war that he had thought out his reasoning. He saw that if Mr. Pitt borrowed the million I have supposed, he would not be able in each succeeding year to pay the interest by taxes, but would have to borrow the money to pay the interest, and then again to borrow for payment of interest upon interest : that in short the loan of a million would increase at compound interest, just like the Indian million.

	Loan.	Indian Investment.
	1,000,000	1,000,000
Interest 1st year	50,000	50,000
„ 2nd year	52,500	52,500
Aggregate at end of 14 years	2,000,000	2,000,000

Besides this, there are all the expenses and possible losses.

A war of a year, There seems therefore, a great difference between a war of a year and a war of many years. In case of a single year's war, even if supported by a loan, it might be wise to continue a sinking-fund, even at some little loss, rather than by breaking its continuity, to run the risk of putting an end to it. The interest on the loan in succeeding years, would no doubt, according to English custom, be paid out of taxes, and therefore out of personal expenditure; that is the loan would be at simple interest: while the sum added during the year's war to the sinking-fund, would in future years accumulate at compound interest.

or of a few years. Even if a war lasted more than a year, but was still a short one, the same rule might be applicable. During the Crimean war, which lasted several years, there was no strain on the resources of the country, or on the credit of Government. There was an annual loan certainly, and it may be said that subsequent loans were contracted partly to pay the interest on the first year's loan: yet remembering the great increase of taxation, and particularly the rise of the income tax to sixteen pence in the £, it may be contended that the interest of all the loans was paid out of the taxes. As soon as peace was restored that was certainly the case: and since that time, we have not only paid the interest, but have repaid the loans themselves.

If we had had such a sinking fund as the one I have imagined, accumulating at 5 per cent., our policy would have been to continue it during the Crimean war. Even if we had had such a fund accumulating at 4 per cent., we might have safely continued it.

But if a long war. But if the Crimean war had continued many years, with an augmenting expenditure, with loans great enough to press on our resources, and with Consols so low as to compel the Government to pay 5 per cent on them, then doubtless, Hamilton's reasoning would be just; and to continue a sinking-fund under such circumstances would have been a mistake.

Final comparison of Price and Hamilton. Here was the difference between Price and Pitt on one side and Hamilton on the other. Price and Pitt hoped for peace as the rule, with war as an occasional exception: after the frequent wars of their century they anticipated a season of repose: had they foreseen a generation of strife, growing out of the most extraordinary revolution on record, and supported by the malignant genius of one of the greatest of imperial soldiers, they would have despaired of their own measures. Hamilton, on the other hand, brought up in a time of war, accustomed to national pressure, to annual loans, and to a high rate of interest, unconsciously regarded war as the rule and peace as the exception : his reasonings apply to his own times : had he foreseen the forty years' peace after Waterloo, he would not have limited his investigations to the results of Pitt's measure, which continued war had spoilt; he would have also inquired what the nation could best accomplish in a state of repose.

England's ill-fortune. It has been the ill-fortune of England that the sinking-fund, which required peace, was begun on the verge of a tremendous war: that the same fund, which peace would have rendered fruitful, was practically abandoned just when war was banished for more than a generation.

IX.

PART II.

MR. PITT'S SINKING-FUND OF 1786.

Sinking-fund 1786: importance of understanding it. The failure of Mr. Pitt's scheme of 1786 has been the stock objection to all recent proposals. To understand that scheme thoroughly, is therefore the fundamental necessity of all our reasonings. If that scheme was essentially fallacious, we learn from it to avoid a similar basis: if it failed merely through unfavourable external circumstances, we may venture once more upon the same course of action, in hopes of better fortune: if the scheme was sound in principle, but had one vicious provision, which the unforeseen and long-continued wars rendered fatal, then we may see how to found a new scheme on the same principle, but free from the mortal taint of the old one. I will therefore now examine the sinking-fund of 1786, by the light of the Indian illustration I have already advanced.

Condemnation by Lord Grenville. If we are to believe Lord Grenville, the scheme was essentially fallacious.*

"Few measures have been more largely applauded than the Act of Parliament which estab-

---

* Essay 1828. 2.

lished, in 1786, a sinking-fund for the reduction of our National Debt. The writer of these pages was himself a party to the too sanguine hopes of those who framed and proposed that law; confidently believing it one of the greatest services which could then be rendered to their country. To that opinion he long adhered; and even now, after the lapse of more than forty years, he feels it still painful to renounce so flattering a persuasion. But the interests of truth and science are paramount to all such considerations; and he who was formerly among the warmest advocates of a sinking-fund, is, on that account, the more strongly bound to avow, on every fit occasion, the distrust which he now entertains of its efficacy and real benefit."

I differ from him. I propose now to give my reasons for agreeing with Mr. Grenville in 1786, and for differing from Lord Grenville in 1828-9.

To me it seems that he was right in 1786, in supporting a scheme founded on a sound basis: that he was wrong in 1829, in distrusting the efficacy of *a* sinking-fund, because the fund of 1786 had been rendered inefficient by long-continued wars, aggravated by one unwise provision in the scheme.

X.

FIRST STAGE.

What the scheme was: 1st stage. LET us recollect what the scheme was. The existing taxation was to be maintained, and a small addition was to be made to it; and it was calculated that there would thus be produced such a surplus, that a million £ a year might be appropriated to reducing the debt. But in order to get the advantage of compound interest, this million was to be paid into the hands of Commissioners, with instructions requiring them to re-invest all the interest they received : that is, the millions paid to the Commissioners were to accumulate at compound interest. To give certainty to the operation, the Commissioners were to receive their annual amounts before there was paid out of the exchequer, anything besides the interest of the national debt; and it was thought that by this means, " the fund would be secured, and no deficiencies in the national revenues could affect it, but such must be separately provided for by Parliament." Besides this annual million, there were certain terminable annuities, the amounts of which as they fell in were to be paid to the Commissioners. It was calculated that at the end of 28 years, the Commissioners would have accumulated such a sum as would yield an annual income of 4 millions £. Mr. Pitt's accuracy in these statements was not disputed by Mr. Fox.

It was founded on surplus income. As I have said before, the foundation of the plan was no legerdemain : it was the appropriation of a surplus revenue of a million sterling, plus terminable annuities as they fell in. Upon this solid basis there were founded hopes of assistance from the action of compound interest; and if peace had continued, the growing prosperity of the nation, and the consequent facility with which the surplus million might have been raised, render it probable that Mr. Pitt's hopes would have been realized. In fact, during the seven years following 1786, the debt was reduced by nearly six millions. So far what was there to lead Mr. Grenville to any well-founded distrust of the efficacy of a sinking fund ?

How the fund might have been invested, Nothing could be more simple than the principle : the Commissioners were to receive and invest at compound interest, a million £ a year at least. But the mode of investment rendered the matter less simple. Let us say that in the seven years between 1786 and 1793 the Commissioners had become possessed of 10 millions £. If they had lent these sums to the East India Company, to be applied to irrigation and public roads, their assets would have been " sums lent to the E. I. Co. on mortgage of their lands, 10 millions £." Parliament and the nation would have understood this.

and was invested. The Commissioners in fact, had no authority to lend money in this way. They were required to buy Government Stocks, and to have them transferred to their names in trust for the nation. This marred the simplicity and perspicuity of the scheme. At the end of the first year the nation owed, suppose 250 millions £, of which however, 1 million £ stood in the names of the Commissioners ; or, what is the same thing, of which 1 million £ " was redeemed." This state of affairs required explanation, and the nation would not be quite sure what was meant : it could not apprehend and hold fast without effort, the fact that nominally the debt remained as before ; but that a million or more stood in the names of a Government department, and was really owing by the nation to itself.

XI.

SECOND STAGE.

2nd Stage: 1793 to 1815. LET us go on to a second stage, that commencing with the long and deadly

French war, which broke out in 1793. In that year we contracted a loan* of 4½ millions £; in 1794 we borrowed† 11 millions £, and at a higher rate‡ than in 1793; and thenceforward till the battle of Waterloo the debt grew fast and yet steadily. The form of a sinking-fund however, was kept up; and it may be true that as special revenue was set apart for it, the taxation may have been increased by means of it, and thus the debt may have been a little kept down. I have already given an account of the various modifications subsequently made in the original sinking-fund : of the one per cent. charged on loans; of the redemption of the Land-Tax; of the renewed efforts after the transient Peace of Amiens; of Lord Henry Petty's elaborate but short-lived plan of 1807. I have also quoted statements from Lord Colchester's Diary: that in 1804 the sum of 1½ millions £ was applied to the sinking-fund, and that the principal actually redeemed since 1786 was more than 100 millions £; and again that in 1811 the principal redeemed was 200 millions £. I have stated that at the end of the war the debt was really about 840 millions, with an annual charge of more than 32 millions £.

Indian Illustration. Suppose now that the Commissioners had invested their moneys in India, and that in 1793 they had had 10 millions £ there. Say that Mr. Pitt in his budget of that year had resolved to apply a million to the sinking-fund, with a proviso that under Mr. Fox's clause of 1786, this million and any other sums not invested, should be lent back again to the Exchequer. The Commissioners' accounts would have stood thus:

---

* Annual Register, 1793, *Chronicle* 221. It was raised in three per cents. at 72, *i.e.*, at about 4¼ per cent. interest. † *Ib.*, 1794, 349.

‡ *Ib.*, 1794, 342. Consols fell from 73⅜ in January, to 63⅝ in October.

1793.
Amount.

Sinking-fund previously	10 millions £
Paid over by the Treasury	1 ,, ,,
One year's interest on 10 millions £	½ ,, ,,
Total	11½ ,, ,,

Assets.

Invested in India	10 millions £
Lent to English Treasury..................	1½ ,, ,,
Total	11½ ,, ,,

1804. Now let us go on to 1804, when we find 1½ million £ applied for the year, and at least 100 millions £ redeemed.

Amount.

Sinking-fund previously	100 millions £
Paid over by the Treasury	1½ ,, ,,
One year's interest on 100 millions £— say at 5 per cent.	5 ,, ,,
Total	106½ ,, ,,

Assets.

Invested in India	10 millions £
Lent to the English Treasury in the years 1793 to 1804	96½ ,, ,,
Total	106½ ,, ,,

1811. The year 1811 shows a similar result on a larger scale, the sum set aside for redemption being 13 millions £, according to Lord Colchester.

Amount.

Sinking-fund previously	200 millions £
Paid over by the Treasury	13 ,, ,,
One year's interest at 5 per cent.	10 ,, ,,
Total	223 ,, ,,

Assets.

Invested in India	10 millions £
Lent to the English Treasury in the years 1793 to 1811	213 ,, ,,
Total	223 ,, ,,

Assume Indian investment withdrawn. We shall get a step nearer to the actual condition of affairs, if we now assume that the Commissioners recalled the 10 millions £ lent to the East India Company, and lent that sum to the home Treasury. The assets would then consist of 223 millions £ owing by the Treasury.

Assets.

Invested in India 0
Lent to the English Treasury in the years
1793 to 1811 .... 223 millions £

XII.

Before and after 1793: in what respects no difference. WE may now see the differences between the sinking-fund before 1793, and the same fund after 1793. During the peace before 1793, additional taxes were levied, and the produce was paid over to the Commissioners; who invested it, hypothetically in India, actually in England; and who held hypothetically Indian securities, actually English Government stock. The Treasury, in fact, owed the Commission what we will call 10 millions £, and paid the interest out of the taxes.

After 1793, during the war, the Treasury went on paying to the Commission, both this interest and additional principal. These sums were invested in Government stocks, just as happened before 1793; with only this difference, that after 1793 the stocks were new ones. In point of *form*, it made no difference as between Treasury and Commission, if the sums thus paid over to the Commission were all borrowed, instead of being raised by taxation.

Both before and after 1793, the sinking-fund in

the hands of the Commissioners went on accumulating at compound interest.

Old and new stocks. Before 1793 the Commissioners used the sums in their hands, to buy on the Stock Exchange portions of old consols or other stocks: after 1793 they received from the Government portions of new consols or other new stocks.

As to form there was no difference: both before and after 1793, the Treasury owed the Commissioners so many millions of money, just as the Treasury owed to the public a far greater number of millions of money; or more exactly, the Treasury was under an agreement to pay certain perpetual annuities to the Commissioners, and a far greater amount of perpetual annuities to the public: the perpetual annuities before 1793 being old ones, after 1793 new ones.

Interest out of taxes or out of loans. The interest before 1793, whether paid to Commissioners or public, was furnished by taxation: after 1793 it was mostly furnished by loans from the public.

Difference to the nation, To the nation there was a vast difference in these two modes: for before 1793, not only there was no increase of debt, but taking Treasury and Commission together, there was a diminution both of debt and of annual charge: after 1793 there was an increase every year both of debt and of annual charge.

and to the Commissioners. To the Commissioners also there was a vast difference; not in form but in reality. In form, the interest was regularly paid, and additional principal was handed over: but in reality, there was created elsewhere a debt equal in amount to the sums paid to the Commissioners; and this creation of debt was of necessity temporary: what was to come after it?

Term wanted: suppose the sinking-fund in abeyance. We want a term to express this difference. To simplify the case, suppose the Treasury had said to the Commission: so long as war continues we can pay you no interest; but we will keep an account of what we should have paid you if peace had been maintained, and all such suspended payments shall accumulate at compound interest, and on the return of peace we will pay you.

Active and passive debt. The Treasury's debt to the Commission before 1793 might then be called *active;* after 1793 it might be called *passive:* just as the Spanish national debts are called active when interest is paid on them, passive when no interest is paid on them.

I have supposed that the Treasury suspended its payments to the Commission during the war, and in this case the debt would have been passive even in form: in reality the Treasury did not suspend those payments during the war, and in form the debt was active.

Taking into account however, the whole finances of the nation, the debt to the Commissioners was passive; because the Treasury borrowed from the public what it paid to the Commissioners, and created debt to the amount of interest paid. We may say therefore, that before 1793 the debt was active, and that after 1793 it was passive.

It may seem that to the Commissioners it was indifferent, whether the sums they received came from taxation or from loans. There was this distinction however: so long as the sums came from taxation they might probably continue to be paid in perpetuity: but when they came from loans they would continue to be paid so long only as loans were made; that is in fact, so long only as the war went on : as soon as peace returned they would have to be paid out of taxation ; and it was doubtful. whether the public would submit to the necessary taxation.

The debt to the Commissioners though in form active was no better than passive ; and on the return of peace it became passive in form as well as reality, because loans ceased, and the public refused the taxation necessary to pay the interest.

Peace. The honest supporters of the sinking-fund hoped that when peace came, the debt owing to the Commissioners would again become active : that the taxpayers would furnish the amount of the interest. If the sinking-fund had been suspended during the war, if it had been maintained at the 10 millions which I assume it to have reached in 1793, the taxpayers in 1815 might have consented to pay the less than half a million required. Unfortunately, the passive debt had grown to such an amount as to require many millions a year of interest, and this the taxpayers declined to furnish.

XIII.

THIRD STAGE.

3rd stage: 1815—29.   THIS explains the phrase used by McCulloch :* " the nominal amount of the sinking-fund began to be diminished after the close of the war " : which means that part of the passive debt owing by the Treasury to the Commissioners, was cancelled.

---

* Adam Smith, 1839, 619.

Honesty of Pitt and others. The proceedings at the close of the war, tested the honesty of Pitt and his successors. McCulloch qualifies this sinking-fund as "a delusive piece of quackery": some may suspect that it was nothing but deliberate trickery; since the actuaries must have known and pointed out to the ministers that the sinking-fund was only a passive debt from department to department. The reply to this suspicion is the fact that after peace was concluded, the debt was acknowledged, and means were taken for meeting the annual charge. In 1819, after our occupation of France had ceased, and the war establishments had been finally reduced, it was proposed to raise 5 millions £ a year for payment of interest due to the Commissioners. This was found too heavy a burden, and after "various modifications" it was enacted that the surplus revenue of whatever amount should constitute the sinking-fund. At the same time, the claim of the Commissioners on the Treasury for hundreds of millions, was abandoned The nation repudiated the passive debt which their right hand owed to their left.

XIV.

CONCLUSION AS TO THE SINKING-FUND OF 1786.

I BELIEVE therefore, that the sinking-fund of 1786, was well fitted to reduce the amount of the national debt; being founded on the provision of an annual million of taxes at least, and the result to 1793 being nearly what was proposed. The failure of the fund I attribute to the long and expensive wars between 1793 and 1815 ; which compelled the nation to borrow every year ; and thus putting an end to the annual surplus of a million, converted the sinking-fund into a passive debt owing by the Treasury to the Commissioners.

Probably the wisest course would have been to leave the 10 millions of stock in the names of the Commissioners, suspending even the payment of interest during the war. On the conclusion of peace the Commissioners might have again begun to claim the interest ; and the nation would not have refused the 300,000 £ or 400,000 £ to which it amounted. The 10 millions £ growing at compound interest, would have now amounted to a considerable sum Besides, the notion of a sinking-fund would not have been discredited ; on the contrary, it would have held its just place in public estimation : other sums would have been added ; the million a year set aside by Mr. Pitt would soon have been resumed, and probably with the growing population and wealth it would have been increased to two or three millions a year. Under these arrangements, with the unexampled continuance of peace, our debt might now have been reduced to two-thirds of its present amount. All was spoiled by attempting too much : by pretending to carry on during war, what peace alone rendered possible.

XV.

CONCLUSIONS.

IN this chapter, I have tried to explain the difficulties which occurred in the previous chapter ; and to do this I have imagined that the Commission established by Mr. Pitt in 1786, applied to public works in India the million annually furnished to them by the British Treasury, and the annual interest they would have received in India. I show that by the year 1870 with interest at 5 per cent., there would have accumulated 1,260 millions £; a sum half as large again as our present debt. This is on the assumption that notwithstanding the war, the million a year was regularly remitted; and also, that by the year 1793, the accumulations from all sources amounted to 10 millions £. I admit that the scheme is purely utopian, and I enter into some particulars merely to give force to the illustration.

I compare the actual proceedings of 1786, with these imaginary proceedings. In Part 7, I point out the disadvantage laboured under by the Commission as to the rate of interest obtained, in consequence of having always to invest in very fluctuating securities, and generally making *bonâ fide* investments when those securities are at the highest. I also trace the effects of Mr. Fox's clause, requiring the Commission to apply money in their possession to take a part of any new loan; the results being that to the public at large the transactions of the Commission became unintelligible, and that the sinking-fund itself ceased to be under the guarantee of public opinion. I show why in my opinion, Dr. Price was wrong in requiring that the sinking-fund should be continued during a time of war and loans, and why Hamilton was right in condemning that practice.

In the Second Part I examine more minutely Mr. Pitt's scheme of 1786. I find that in its first stage, between 1786 and 1793, it was an honest sinking-fund, founded on an annual surplus, which surplus was taken every year out of the Budget, and placed in the hands of a Commission, for accumulation at compound interest. As to the second stage beginning with the war loans of 1793, when the debt had been reduced by about 6 millions £, I inquire what results would have followed if the Commission had invested its funds in India. I then go on to 1804, when the sinking-fund amounted to about 100 millions £, and to 1811, when it amounted to about 200 millions £. I ask what would have been the condition of our finances if peace had been made in 1811; and I reply that the Government would have owed to *the public* about 600 millions £, and to the Commission about 200 millions £. I then inquire what was the difference between the 6 millions £ sinking-fund before 1793, and the 200 millions £ sinking-fund in 1811. I find that before 1793, the debt was an *active* one : that from 1793 to 1811, the debt was a *passive* one ; the interest either not being paid to the Commission, or only paid by contracting a debt elsewhere : that on the hypothesis of a peace and a cessation of loans in 1811, it was necessary to make the debt to the Commission again active; that is, without borrowing, to pay the Commission the annual interest on 200 millions £, amounting permanently to far more than 6 millions £ a year. I give reasons for believing that this was really intended by Pitt and his successors, whose good faith in the matter is therefore not necessarily impugned.

CHAPTER IV.

PROGRESS OF DEBT AND REPAYMENT:
BRITISH AND FOREIGN.

I.

British Progress unsatisfactory. I WILL now give a short statement, in general terms, of the progress of our debt since its commencement at the Revolution. In our earlier history we find loans made to the Sovereign, not to the nation: for example; the City lent Henry VII. £4,000, which sum was punctually repaid * Queen Elizabeth's exactness in repayment is also mentioned by Strype.†

I will add a few figures as to the debt and the efforts for repayment of other countries. The English pride themselves on their political and financial prudence: I fear that the following tables will not confirm their self-laudation.

Debt has outrun prosperity. The prosperity of Great Britain during the last hundred years, is, on so large a scale, unexampled; while its population has multiplied, its wealth has increased still faster: yet its National Debt has augmented in a still greater ratio; and in times of peace little has been done to pay off the war debts.

---

* Bacon's Henry VII., Ed. 1852, p. 362.
† Strype's Annals, Ed. 1725, 2. 102.

1689 *to* 1866. The following are the amounts given in a Parliamentary Paper 19 July, 1858. (443).

1691.	3 millions.
1702.	13 ,,
1714.	36 ,,
1727.	52 ,,
1763.	133 ,,
1775.	127 ,,
1786.	246 ,,
1793.	240 ,,
1815.	860 ,,
1838.	787 ,,
1855.	802 ,,
1857.	832 ,,
1861.	818 ,,
1866.	803 ,,

It will be seen that the amount is now larger than it was in 1838 : in the 28 years we had one war, that with Russia : the Indian mutiny cost us nothing : at the end of the generation we had increased our debt instead of lessening it.

The annual charge lowered. The annual charge indeed, is much less than it was.

In 1816 it was	32 millions.
,, 1838 it was only	29¼ ,,
,, 1860-1 ,, ,,	28¼ ,,
It then fell to	26¼ ,,
It is now	26 ,,

How ? partly by fall of interest : partly by cessation of terminable annuities. A considerable part of this reduction has been caused by a fall in the rate of interest, a small part by diminution of principal. The sudden reduction in 1861, was caused by the falling in of a large amount of terminable annuities. Part of the previous annual payment was in fact a sinking-fund. Even now we are paying in the same way more than a million a year beyond 3 per cent. interest and cost of management ; and this also is a sinking-fund.

1856—66 and 1838—66. The most unsatisfactory circumstance is, that the debt is larger than it was in 1855 : that is, that during eleven years we did not quite repay the loans we contracted. The period has been one of singular prosperity: there was commercial disorder in 1857, but it lasted only a short time: nearly each year the Chancellor of the Exchequer has had to announce an income beyond his estimate, through the constantly increasing produce of the taxes. Other nations, seeing our success, are strongly imitating those free trade measures which they believe to have produced it, and most of those imitations add to our commerce and our resources. Yet with all this flow of national income, we had not up to 1866, paid back the money we borrowed in the previous 9 years. Reduction of expenditure, reduction of taxation: anything but systematically paying our debts.

II.

We approve the sinking-funds of others: the United States.

WHILE we thus shut our eyes to our own duty, we are ready to admire and applaud other nations who perform theirs. The United States between 1861 and 1865, incurred a debt of which the interest is nearly as much as ours: as soon as the war ceased, the ministry and the newspapers declared the nation ready to pay off the whole principal within the next generation: we strongly approved and half believed. If such a resolution is good for them, why not for us?

What the United States have done: apparently,

At starting, the United States did wonderful things. Peace was concluded in 1865: by the 1st August of the next year, it was announced that 25 millions £ had been paid off. Sanguine men began to calculate how few years would at this rate discharge the whole; and there were smiles on American faces at the thought of their superiority to the effete Europeans, whose national debts never are discharged.

really. But a little investigation diminished the wonder and the hopes. In the early part of 1865, the Government, whatever they might anticipate, could not trust in the termination of hostilities: they might expect that Sherman would march across the Southern territory to the Atlantic; that Richmond would fall; that Lee would surrender; that Stephens would be their prisoner: but their "ninety days'" boasting had so often been falsified that they continued to prepare for further war, by strictly levying their taxes and by raising loans. Thus, when peace suddenly came, they had large sums of money in hand, and with these they repaid part of the loans. They had the pleasure of dazzling the world by announcing the discharge of 25 millions £ of debt in one year; but the feat could not be repeated.

Still bent on repayment, as formerly. Still however, they seem bent on repayment: they want to do what they have done before: the Federal Government has more than once discharged all its liabilities: it is the separate States, Pennsylvania for a time, and Mississippi permanently, that repudiated their engagements.

Difficulties: charges are perhaps 30,000,000 £. The American people however, begin to find that the civil contest has left among them the same evils that Europeans have suffered formerly: they have discovered that even democratic freedom and unlimited territory leave men exposed to the consequences of profuse expenditure. Charges on a debt cannot be paid without taxation: the interest and pensions they have to supply annually are said to be no less than 30 millions £.* It is true that the principal of the debt is nothing like in proportion to this; being on the 1st April, 1867, only 2,523 millions of dollars, or rather more than 500 millions £; supposing that all of it will be paid, or permanently assumed, as if it had been borrowed with the dollar worth 4s. 2d. as it was before the war. The principal is only five-eighths of ours. Besides this however, it is contended† that we ought to take into account the debts "incurred by individual States, Counties, and Towns, for bounties and other war purposes;" amounting according to one writer to 300 millions £, though other persons say this is a gross exaggeration. The purchase of the Russian territory henceforth to be called *Alaska*, the negociation for the Danish islands, and the rumoured offer of Cuba by Spain, are unfavourable to the declared resolution to vigorously diminish these alarming liabilities. A punster might suggest a propriety in the new name, Alaska.

Disturbance of production. For the present also, the productive powers of the Union are in disorder; as might have been expected after such a sudden, monstrous struggle, ending in the forcible emancipation of four millions of slaves, and the destruction of a great part of the capital of those who should have been their employers. In 1819, four years after European peace had been concluded, the distress in England was frightful. The commercial relations which had adapted themselves to twenty years of war, had to be modified: as Robert Owen said,

---

* *Economist*, 27th April, 1867, 470, col. 1.
† *Economist*, May 25, 1867, p. 585, col. 2.

"War, our great customer, is dead." A similar dislocation has taken place in America.

Account by the Standard. The *Economist* of 27th April, 1867, quotes from the *Standard*, the following remarkable account :—

"Trade has not been so dull since 1857 as at the present time. The warehouses are filled with idle dealers, the shops with idle clerks, the streets with idle mechanics. The spring business is already over. The merchants are preparing for a storm. The people are wearing their old clothes, drawing on the Savings' Banks, and giving another turn to the economical screw. Rents and provisions are enormously high; and although dress goods are cheaper than at the same time last year, the people have no inclination to buy. I am confident that a month will not elapse before the failure of some of our oldest mercantile houses is chronicled. The depression is noticeable in every department of trade. The newspaper proprietors, with one exception, are drawing on their capital. The business of the railway companies is much smaller than at the corresponding period last year. The woollen and cotton mills are running upon short time, and some of them will soon suspend work altogether. And, a worse sign, the clamours of the Gold Room and the Stock Exchange are more furious than ever. People are everywhere grumbling about the *high taxes*. The nigger question is being lost sight of in the financial question. A hundred circumstances betoken great uneasiness in the public mind—trouble in the present and fears for the future. The statements of the Secretary of the Treasury are satisfactory, as showing a reduction in the public debt, and a heavy balance of gold in the Treasury; but when the bills of expenses incurred by Congress become due, the showing will have a different colour. We have wantonly deprived ourselves of the benefit of the resources of the most fertile half of our domain. While adding to the burdens of the North, we have paralysed industry in the South.

"During the war, we burned the candle at both ends. The attention of the crowd was directed to the illumination. Engaged in a gigantic war her children were never before so prosperous. Fortunes were never before made so rapidly. The mechanic was never before so busy and so well paid. So rich were the Americans that they were able to make a free gift of hundreds of millions of dollars to their volunteer soldiers. .   .   .   .   .   .

"All this has changed. The army has disappeared. The hundreds of workshops where army clothes and munitions were manufactured are closed. The working men have used up their savings of paper. To be sure the paper dollar is, when compared with the gold dollar, worth more than it was a year ago, but it will buy less than then"

Disappointment to the Americans. All this is a great disappointment to those Americans who believed that a national debt would scarcely be felt in their great country. The following summary of the nonsense that was talked, appeared on the 27th July, 1865, in a Bristol paper of which I have lost the name.

"Mr. Jay Cooke, the financial agent of the United States Government who is charged with the issue of each successive loan, has set up it as an authorized dogma, that a national debt is a national blessing, and the New York press generally support him in this view. The *Journal of Commerce*, however, and the *New York Commercial Advertiser* dispute the new theory, and the latter, while protesting against the

R

method employed to attract subscribers by the aid of
'advertisements like those of patent medicine vendors
or of the managers of circuses and menageries,'
asks why, if a national debt is such a blessing, have
the American people always insisted on economy in
the adminstration of their Federal Government;
and why, instead of a debt of six hundred millions
sterling, should they not at once seek to have one of
six thousand millions? Mr. Jay Cooke, in a series
of propositions, stated with all the pomp of mathe-
matical precision, informs the people that the
advantages of a national debt will be that the larger
portion of its annual responsibility will fall in America
as in England, upon the proprietary rather than the
operative classes; that by the abundance of capital
it creates 'it will probably transfer the workshops
of the world from England to America;' and,
lastly, that, as it will render requisite a high tariff on
foreign manufactures, it will be a wall to prevent the
domestic manufactures of the country from being
washed away by importations. 'Protection and
Excise,' it is proclaimed, 'are essential to each
other. Both are necessary to sustain the National
Debt. It will be seen from this that the United
States is moving in the wrong direction.
England goes in for free-trade; the United States
demand protection; England is very glad to have
her debt reduced if it is only to the extent of ten
millions; the United States says a debt is a blessing
that will ultimately resuscitate American finance,
consolidate national manufactures, and enable
America in general to whip all creation. This is
an excellent view to take—so long as the loans are
wanted."

It must be remembered that just as much nonsense has been talked in England. So great a

123

genius as Coleridge maintained that taxation was not the evil it appeared. I am not aware whether he published his opinion ; but if he did not, many others were less prudent.

Dearness, from taxation, But why the gold dollar should buy so little, requires explanation ; which however, is the very simple one of the pressure of internal taxation.*

on everything made: " The American law took no notice of the division of labour ; such a law could not, indeed, make a distinction between articles sold to a manufacturer and articles sold to a consumer; it would have been baffled by wholesale evasion if it had attempted a distinction. It taxed all 'makings' 6 per cent." The Commissioners say,

often taxed twice over. " Under the operation of this law, the Government now levies and collects from 8 to 15 per cent., and even in some instances 20 per cent., on almost every finished industrial product. In order to fully understand the reasons of such conclusions, it must be borne in mind that but comparatively few products of manufacturing industry come to the consumer as the result of one process, but that the finished product is almost always an aggregate of several distinct and separate manufacturing processes." After mentioning an umbrella as an article of which the parts are made by several manufacturers, and which therefore pays 6 per cent. first on each part, and then 6 per cent. again as a complete umbrella, the Commissioners go on :—

Shipbuilding an example. " The effect of this upon such a trade as shipbuilding is obvious. A ship is a far more composite article than an umbrella. The

---

* *Economist*, April 20, 1867. 438.

frame of the ship may be cut out and put together in the building yard; but the iron, the yellow metal, the masts, the sails, the spars, the cordage, and much else, must all be bought elsewhere; it is what Americans might call 'an assembled article'; and upon every item so collected, *two* taxes at least are paid—one by the seller, of whom the shipbuilder buys, and another by the shipbuilder himself. The new taxation of America has therefore, a most sure tendency to drive capital from a complex manufacture like shipbuilding to simple manufactures which are only charged once, and agriculture which is not charged at all."

Compared with the former Spanish tax on sales. This American tax, levied again and again on the same article, too nearly resembles that Spanish *alcavala* to which, says* Adam Smith, "Ustaritz imputes the ruin of the manufactures of Spain." The motive indeed, was different in the two countries. In America it was a resolution to maintain the greatness of the Union, at whatever present inconvenience. But in Spain it was an attempt to increase the royal revenue at the expense of mercantile profit.

"In *consequence of the notion that duties upon consumable goods were taxes upon the profits of merchants, those duties have, in some countries, been repeated upon every successive sale of the goods. If the profits of the merchant importer or merchant manufacturer were taxed, equality seemed to require that those of all the middle buyers who intervened between either of them and the consumer should likewise be taxed. The famous alcavala of Spain seems to have been established upon this principle. It was at first a tax of ten per cent.,

---

* Adam Smith, Book v., chap. 2. McCulloch. Edition, 1839., pa. 407.

afterwards of fourteen per cent., and is at present only six per cent. upon the sale of every sort of property, whether moveable or immoveable ; and it is repeated every time the property is sold. The levying of this tax requires a multitude of revenue officers sufficient to guard the transportation of goods not only from one province to another but from one shop to another. It subjects not only the dealers in some sorts of goods, but those in all sorts, every farmer, every manufacturer, every merchant and shopkeeper, to the continual visits and examination of the tax-gatherers. Through the greater part of a country in which a tax of this kind is established, nothing can be produced for distant sale. The produce of every part of the country must be proportioned to the consumption of the neighbourhood."

Accounts for the high prices The American tax, being levied only on things made, and not on raw produce nor on sales of goods, is doubtless much less oppressive than the alcavala. But it is quite sufficient, supported as it is by high import duties, to account for the present prices of commodities, which are extravagantly high, even after allowing for the fact that it takes 135 or 140 paper dollars to buy 100 gold dollars.

actually prevailing. "Take* the condition of the ordinary working man—a carpenter let us say. While at work, he receives, if an adept in his business, three dollars and a half a day (14s. 7d. if the dollar were a gold one). Before the war, he thought himself fortunate if he obtained one dollar and a half a day (6s. 3d.) But he now pays 6 dols. a week for the rent of three rooms ; before the war, he paid a weekly rent of $1\frac{1}{2}$ dol. or 2 dols. for the same rooms.

---

* *Economist*, April 27, 1867. 470, col. 2.

For flour of medium quality, he now pays, if he buys it by the barrel, 12 dols. to 13 dols. the barrel; before the war he rarely paid more than $5\frac{1}{2}$ dols. or 6 dols. for the same quality. The beef that he buys for his Sunday dinner costs him now 18 cents a pound; in 1860, beef of as good a quality brought 6 to 10 cents a pound. Potatoes now sell for 1 dol. a bushel; before the war they were dear at 20 cents a bushel."

One-fourth depreciation. From these prices, if we take the old valuation of a cent for a halfpenny, a fourth must be deducted for depreciation of the currency: the price of gold being 135; *i.e*, it being necessary to give 135 paper dollars for a thing worth 100 gold dollars, or fully one-third more. At the same time, we must deduct one-fourth from the wages quoted.

Comparison with England, 1816. It is an interesting question, whether the Americans will be able to maintain any considerable sinking-fund, under these peculiar circumstances. A comparison of what happened in England at the end of the last war, will not help us much. In the year that followed the peace we had great distress: all the trading channels formed by twenty years of war were for the time obstructed. Prices, no doubt, were inflated by the depreciation of our paper, when compared with gold: but this had taken place before the peace; and after 1815 there was a general fall. A great meeting was held in London in 1816, to consider what could be done to relieve the general distress.* "Barns and farmyards were full, and warehouses were weighed down with all manner of productions, and prices fell much below the cost at which the articles could be produced."

---

* Life of R. Owen, 93.

Cessation of our war, 1815. "The* war was a great and most extravagant customer to farmers, manufacturers, and other producers of wealth, and many during this period became very wealthy. The expenditure of the last year of the war for this country alone, was one hundred and thirty millions sterling, or an excess of eighty millions sterling over the peace expenditure. And on the day on which peace was signed, *this great customer of the producers died;* and prices fell as the demand diminished, until the prime cost of the articles required for war could not be obtained"

English depreciation of currency. The depreciation of the currency during the late American war, was not new. To say nothing of the French assignats, or the colonial currency of the American revolutionary war, English bank-notes fell so far below their nominal value between 1809 and 1815, that they were for a time nearly as much depreciated as American greenbacks are at present. But after the peace they soon recovered themselves by the reappearance of gold, and the determination of Parliament to resume cash payments.†

Cash payments resumed, & a large sinking-fund begun. Notwithstanding this difficulty, the nation was bent on diminishing its debt; and in 1819, while still suffering from depression of trade, from resumption of

---

* Life of R. Owen, 96.

† I do not mean to put the English and the American depreciation in the same category in every respect. The greenbacks are *certainly* depreciated through excess: our currency was *perhaps* depreciated through scarcity of gold: if so, it is more accurate to say, not that the notes were depreciated, but that gold was enhanced. At present, the weight of authority, and, I think, of argument, is in favour of this opinion, once deemed worthy of an *auto da fe*, that the apparent depreciation of paper was a real enhancement of gold; caused first, by the demand for military purposes, secondly, by the hoarding which from the time of Popys until the present century, has regularly followed European disturbances.

cash payments, and from great political discontents, it determined to raise so large a sum as 5 millions £ a year for a sinking fund ; a noble resolution, which unfortunately failed in the execution.

What will the United States do? It will be very interesting to watch the future proceedings of the United States. They too, are bent on paying off their debt; as the Federal Government has already done more than once in its history : they have imposed an excise duty of 3 cents. (1½d.) per lb. on cotton wool* ; they are submitting to that tax on all things made, which seems to interfere so much with their industry : they continue the oppressive income-tax. But the tax on cotton is protested against : the tax on manufactures can hardly be expected to hold its ground : we Europeans can with difficulty believe that the income-tax will continue very long. Determined as they are to pay, they may be unable to resist the force of circumstances ; and the necessity of restoring commercial prosperity may compel them to postpone their efforts. Besides, they have still to take the steps necessary to withdraw their inconvertible paper.

III.

France: writings on. EXCELLENT articles on national debts will be found in many French works : particularly in the " †Dictionnaire de l'Économie Politique ;" and in the very readable treatises of M. Michel Chevalier.‡

---

* Reduced after Sept. 1, 1867, to 2½ cents. (1¼d.)
† Dict. de l'Écon. Pol., 2nd Ed. 1. 512. *Ib.* 842. *Ib.* 684.
‡ M. Michel Chevalier, " Cours d'Économie Pol." 1. 97.

Debt ancient, France began a national debt very early. "On sait par un règlement que fit Sully, en 1604, qu'on payait encore à ce moment des rentes créés, en 1375, par Charles V.; ce sont les plus anciennes dont, en France, nous ayons connaissance. Après Charles V., François Ier. emprunta pour porter la guerre en Italie, puis pour acquitter sa rançon, et c'est ce dernier emprunt qui a été l'origine de la vénalité des charges."

but far heavier in modern times. But it is in modern times that it has become formidable.

"Le crédit public n'existe dans de larges proportions et sur des fondemens certains, que depuis une époque assez rapprochée de nous. On pourrait dire qu'il est contemporain de la Révolution française, quoique la dette anglaise fût déjà d'un milliard près d'un siècle auparavant. Mais c'est à partir de la Révolution française que le crédit public a reçu généralement une organisation régulière. Sans doute avant ce temps des gouvernements avaient eu recours à des emprunts. La république romaine emprunta pour résister aux coups que lui portait Annibal. François Ier. avait créé des rentes. Louis XIV. et Louis XV. avaient fortement endetté l'état, et toutes le grandes monarchies avaient suivi la même voie, en vertu de ce penchant qu'avaient ces gouvernements sans contrôle à dépenser toutes les sommes qu'ils pouvaient se procurer par quelque moyen que ce fût. Toutefois, les lois du crédit public et ses règles suprêmes n'ont été établies en théorie et en pratique que depuis les dernières années du dix-huitième siècle."

Le Grand-Livre. During the Revolution of '89, all the debts of the nation were consolidated, purged, and inscribed in a *Grand-Livre*.

"La loi du 24 août 1793, rendue sur le mémorable rapport de Cambon, ordonna une liquidation générale de tous les titres à la charge de l'état ainsi que l'inscription des créances définitivement reconnues sur un registre unique qui reçut le nom de *grand-livre*. Elle prescrivit également qu'après l'inscription de toute la dette perpétuelle, il serait fait une copie de ce registre, comme une précaution contre les conséquences d'un incendie."

The revolution and Napoleon. The revolution of '89 and the wars that followed, made regular government impossible; and without regular government and unimpeachable credit, loans, if they can be had at all, must be had on severe terms. Napoleon however, refused to borrow largely: he preferred the more immoral mode of requiring war to bear its own expenses; that is of making requisitions on invaded countries.

After the peace of 1815. After 1815, the restored Bourbons borrowed considerably. The heavy fine levied on France by the Allies, caused loans in 1817 and 1818 of 28 millions £. In 1823 again there was the Spanish war, and a loan of 16 millions £. The following are the loans from 1815 to 1837.*

AFTER THE RESTORATION.			UNDER THE ORLEANS DYNASTY.		
1815 May and June	1½	millions £.	1830	3	millions £
1816	2¼	,,	1831	6	,,
1817 }	28	,,	1832	6	,,
1818 }			1835	5	,,
1821	9	,,	1836	2	,,
1823	16	,,	1837	4	,,
	57			26	

---

* Dict. de l'Écon. Pol., 2nd Ed. I. 684.

The interest at different periods has been as follows* :—

ON THE FUNDED DEBT.

UNDER THE ELDER BOURBONS.

1814, 1st April .... 2¼ millions £.
1830, 1st August............... 8 ,,

UNDER THE ORLEANS DYNASTY.

1848, 1st March .... 10 ,,

DURING THE REPUBLIC.

1852, 1st January .... 10 ,,

UNDER LOUIS NAPOLEON.

1861, 1st January .... 14 ,,
1862, 1st January .... 14 ,,
1863, 1st January .... 15 ,,
1864, 1st January .... 15 ,,

A very large sum† has to be added to these amounts, for the unfunded debt: in 1862, no less than 4 millions £; making the annual charge 18 millions £ instead of 14.

Reduction of French interest. As in England, so in France, the rate of interest has been much lowered from time to time: for example, in 1825,‡ M. Villèle reduced a 5 per cent. stock to a 3 per cent., while in England there was a reduction from 5 to 4 per cent., and from 4 to 3½.

Confusion caused by a nominal sinking-fund. In 1816 a sinking-fund was commenced in France, on the principle of Mr. Pitt's English one. It has long ceased to produce any effect but that

---

* See the French " *Annuaire* do l'Écon. Pol. et Stat."
† *Economist*, 999, 1152.
‡ Juglar, " Crises Commerciales, 1862," 19, 20; and Maclaren, 162.

of creating confusion in the accounts. It is owing to this, that the annual interest the French have to pay, is stated at several millions more one day than it is the next day. Thus, as shown by the English *Economist*,* in 1862, the annual interest appeared to be nearly 24 millions £: but the income of the sinking fund was nearly 6 millions £ : the real annual interest on funded and unfunded debt together was therefore about 18 millions £, instead of 24; or fully six millions sterling less than ours.

How it appears in French Budget. The following quotation† will show the form which the French sinking fund has now assumed:—

" *Budget de l'Amortissement.*"

" Ce projet de budget diffère peu de celui qui a été voté en 1866. Cependant il ne propose ancune aliénation, *ni coupes extraordinaires de bois.*

" Il alloue, comme pour 1867, 31 millions, appli- cables aux garanties d'intérêts dues aux compagnies de chemins de fer. Or, l'augmentation considérable du trafic de ces chemins aura pour consequence, d'un côté, d'atténuer la garantie due par le Trésor, et par suite la dépense prévue ; de l'autre, d'élever les recettes de la Caisse d'amortissement par l'accroisse- ment qu'éprouvera l'impôt du dixième.

" Cette éventualité, si elle se réalise, rendra plus importantes les *ressources destinées au rachat des rentes*, mais sans en tenir compte, la somme dont on disposera pour cet objet sera supérieure au *minimum* de 20 millions fixé par la loi."

---

* *Economist*, Oct. 18, 1862, 1152.

† " Journal des Économistes," Janvier, 1867, 129.

Augmented French prosperity: slow increase of population. Great as has been the addition to the debt, the power to bear the burden has grown apparently still faster. It is true that the people multiply very slowly: a fact that dismays those who regard military glory as the highest necessity of the nation; but which rather rejoices those who are bent on peaceful pursuits, and who see that an increased production with a stationary population gives a larger share of subsistence to each individual. Standing still however, is abhorrent to publicists.

* " Or nous avons malheureusement à montrer que notre puissance relative, basée sur le chiffre de notre population, va en s'affaiblissant depuis l'ère des grandes armées permanentes, et que le projet d'organisation militaire, tel qu'il paraît avoir été conçu, aboutirait directement sous ce rapport à la ruine de la France. Un grand fait indéniable, indiscutable, domine toute la question : notre population s'accroît en nombre avec une lenteur fatale ; celle des grands états voisins augmente avec une rapidité consolante pour l'humanité, inquiétante toutefois pour l'avenir de la puissance française."

Then follows a comparison of different countries. With the exception of Austria, Wurtemberg, the Romagna, the Marches, Umbria, and the ancient duchies of Parma, Modena, and Placentia, almost all the European states double their population much faster than France : Greece in 44 years ; England in 52 ; † Prussia in 54 ; Norway and Spain in 57 ; Denmark and Sweden in 63 ; Russia in 66 : whereas at the present rate of progress, France will not double in less than 198 years. The particular con-

---

* *Revue des deux Mondes*, 15th May, 1867. 463.
† That is England and Wales, not including Scotland and Ireland.

sequence which incenses the writer, is this: that fifty years hence, France will have only 47 millions to oppose to 67 millions in Prussian Germany. This interesting topic will be found fully discussed by the Paris Society of Political Economy, at a sitting when Mr. Gladstone and Mr. Cardwell were present.*

Growing French wealth. If the opulence of France had not advanced faster than its population, the prospect would be dark: but the immense addition to the exports, and the augmented productiveness of the taxes, prove that the reverse is true. It is obvious too, how this increased wealth has arisen.†

Productive public works. "Cette activité nouvelle s'est manifestée, surtout depuis 1830, par d'immenses travaux publics qui, exécutés cette fois sur tous les points du territoire, ont laissé bien loin derrière eux ceux qui les avaient précédés. 125,000 kilomètres de chemins nouveaux ont été ouverts, de nombreux canaux ont été creusés, des rivières améliorées, des ports créés ou perfectionnés; 9,000 kilomètres de chemins de fer sont venus s'ajouter à ce beau réseau; 7,000 autres se construisent et doivent s'achever successivement. Par suite de ce progrès constant des communications, des échanges jusqu'alors inconnus se sont établis, les conditions du travail ont changé de fond en comble, la production a conquis une puissance qui semble braver tous les obstacles: les révolutions, les guerres, les disettes, les épidémies, tous ces fléaux, autrefois mortels, peuvent désormais l'arrêter dans ses progrès, mais non la réduire."

---

* *Journal des Économistes*, February, 1867, 307. See also the same publication, January, 1867, 110; and February, 327 and 342.

† L. de Lavergne, *Économie Rurale*, 1866, 47.

French Local Debts. Besides the general taxation, France raises considerable sums locally; though as it is presumed, her centralized government prevents the provincial imposts generally from approaching those of Great Britain, where they certainly amount to a fourth of what Parliament levies.

That of Paris. Of late years however, the reconstruction of Paris has more than made up for this difference: the sums expended, as we have recently learnt, having gone beyond the wildest conjectures.

In 1864 indeed, we were told by Mr. Tite,* that the *Rue de Rivoli*, instead of paying its own expenses, as sanguine persons supposed it would, by the increased value of the surplus land taken, cost, after deducting the price of resales of such land, no less than 3 millions £,† of which the city of Paris had to pay nearly a million £: further, that the city had to pay for the *Halles Centrales* another million, and nearly as much for the *Boulevard Sebastopol*.

In 1865, the trustworthy *Economist*‡ informed us that Paris had so large a revenue as $4\frac{1}{2}$ millions £, and that it proposed to borrow at one time 10 millions £. The year afterwards, 1866, we learnt on the highest French authority,§ that after this loan of 10 millions £ had been contracted, the whole debt was 20 millions £. In the next year, 1867, the public was amazed on learning‖ that the Crédit-foncier had advanced in little more than a year, $11\frac{1}{2}$ millions £. It has turned out since that time,¶ that the annual budget is nearer 10 millions £ than $4\frac{1}{2}$ as was formerly said: that a loan has been

---

* *Statistical Journal*, 27. 378.   † Not francs but pounds sterling.
‡ 15th July, 1865. 849 col. 2. (rate of interest nearly $4\frac{1}{4}$ per cent.)
§ *Revue des deux Mondes*, 1st August, 1866, 649.
‖ *Ib.* April 15, 1867. 1043.   ¶ *Economist*, 1268. 1417.

contracted with the Crédit-foncier, of either 15, 16, or 18 millions £;* and that the whole debts approach 40 millions £. It turns out also that the Prefect of the Seine, who bears the responsibility, has expended on these reconstructions, 21 millions £ beyond what his legal powers authorized : that the vast debt has been nearly all contracted since the revolution of 1848 : further,† that the 20 years' improvements have cost about a milliard of francs (40 millions £) ; and that therefore, they have nearly all been carried out with borrowed money.

Marseilles: prosperity. Marseilles again has pursued a career of improvements, which to sober-minded Englishmen seems alarming. The French are proud of their great seaport, and of its rapid increase. The population at different periods has been as follows.‡

1811—96,271
1846—183,000
1866—300,000§ } With a provision of room for 100,000 more.

The writer of the article on which I rely, states that America alone has the privilege of such rapid expansion ; but he is evidently ignorant of English growth.

In 55 years Marseilles increased to more than three times its original population ; therefore in 60 years it would increase to *less* than fourfold ; but in 60 years Birmingham increased to *more* than fourfold ; Manchester to more than $4\frac{1}{2}$-fold ; Wolverhampton to nearly 5-fold ; Liverpool to nearly $5\frac{1}{2}$-fold.‖

---

* *Economist*, 1267. 1382; *Journal des Écon.* Dec. 1867. 437; *Economist*, 1268, 1417.
† *Revue des deux Mondes*, 72. 1027 ; *Pall Mall*, Dec. 20 and 24, 1867.
‡ *Revue des deux Mondes*, 1st August, 1866. 621.
§ According to the *Pall Mall Gazette*, 22nd October, 1866, pa. 4, the population was in 1836, 362,325 ; in 1866, 547,887. Probably some *district* is meant : no authority is given. ‖ *Statistical Journal*, March, 1866. 103.

Outlay in Marseilles, The increase of Marseilles however, has been very great; and is dwarfed only by comparison with that of American and English towns. It began its course of expenditure nearly thirty years ago, when it had no debt. The first great work was the " Canal de la Durance," for supplying fresh water. At the commencement of the undertaking, in 1840,* the town revenues amounted to 120,000 £, but by 1847 they had risen to 170,000 £ : in 1866 they were† 420,000 £, of which the *octroi* furnished 1 £ per head of population.‡ The canal and other improvements had cost up to 1866, 29 millions £, of which sum only 3 millions £ has been paid by the general government. An outlay of 26 millions £ in 26 years, or a million a-year, is worthy of the United States. In English towns of equal size, a fourth part of the sum would be thought alarming,

and Debt. The debt in 1866‡ was more than 4 millions £, much less certainly, than one would have anticipated.

Compare with Liverpool. A Frenchman might perhaps rebut any imputation of extravagance, by reminding us that the debt of Liverpool has risen to 16½ millions £. But in fact, of this large sum, 15 millions £ has been borrowed for enterprises that yield a money income: viz., 13 millions £ for docks, and 2 millions £ for waterworks; leaving only a million and a half as a charge on the local taxes; a burden not at all out of proportion to the population and means of the borough. The 15 millions laid out on the docks and waterworks, are as far from distressing the inhabitants, as the same amount invested in a railway.

---

* *Revue des deux Mondes*, 1st Aug., 1866. 643.   † *Ib.*, 649.

‡ " Dict. de l'Écon. Pol.," II., 288.

T

Conclusion as to France. On the whole, France has no reason to be proud of her financial management. In 1819, even after the European demands had been satisfied, the debt was but a trifle, which might have easily been paid off, and certainly in times of peace need not have been increased. But each new dynasty, unsettled, and fearing another revolution, has been too intent on the present to provide for future generations. The elder Bourbons, with a nation impoverished by wars and conscriptions, may be excused for having added a considerable amount: the Orleans dynasty in its eighteen years of power, need not have followed this example: but it is the present Emperor, who, departing from the practice of his uncle, has done the greatest mischief, by borrowing without stint.

Other European countries. A table of the debts of other European countries, is given in a recent publication :—*

			£.		Per head of population. £. s. d.
Great Britain	1865		808 millions		27 16 0
France	1865		510 ,,		14 7 2
Russia	1865		264 ,,		3 11 1
Prussia	1864		42 ,,		2 3 3
Austria	1863		247 ,,		6 14 10
Italy	1865		176 ,,		7 19 5
Spain	1866		164 ,,		10 4 6
Portugal	1865-66		42 ,,		9 11 6
Holland	1864		85 ,,		23 1 4
Belgium	1864		25 ,,		5 6 0
Denmark	1866		11 ,,		4 0 0
Sweden	1864-66		3 ,,		0 14 5
Norway	1863-66		2 ,,		1 1 6
Turkey	1865		50 ,,		1 8 0
Greece	1864		11 ,,		9 15 3

Only an approximation. These figures however, are only an approximation to the truth. I have

---

* "Annals of British Legislation." April, 1867. 209.

shown in the case of France, that to arrive at the real amount, we must first, from the funded debt deduct the large sinking-fund, and then add the unfunded debt. In this list the French debt is set down as having been two years ago 540 millions £: elsewhere* I learn that a year later, the excess of expenditure has brought it up to only 483 millions £, nearly 60 millions £ less.

In M. Maurice Block's† " Puissance Comparée " a similar schedule is given; and Russia is there set down at half the debt of my schedule; Greece at one-third.

V.

Prussia. THE two most remarkable cases are those of Prussia and Holland. Prussia has followed to a wonderful degree, the frugal maxims and the careful administration of Frederick: this constancy has made her poverty‡ predominate over the resources of her rivals. The smallness of her national debt is astonishing; since it is only per head of population one-twelfth that of Great Britain, and in absolute amount one-twelfth that of France.

---

* *Pall Mall Gazette*, 22 Dec., 1866. 2 col.
† French edition, published at Gotha, 1862. P. 164.
‡ Grant Duff, 243. It appears however, that Mr. Grant Duff has underrated the present resources of Prussia. The *Revue des deux Mondes*, (71. pp. 47, 58, and 61), says that though up to 1840 great agricultural distress prevailed, and land was worth but little, in consequence of the desolating wars before 1815, and of the disturbance caused by the abolition of serfdom; yet that since that time, and especially of late years, much progress has been made in the productiveness and prosperity of agriculture. The increase too, of Berlin, and other great towns of the Zollverein, is set down as prodigious. —(*Pall Mall Gazette*, Oct. 18, 1867, page 7.)

Former repudiation, In comparing other countries with England however, we ought to recollect that we always acknowledge the whole of the debt we have ever contracted : the wonderful expansion of population and wealth, having enabled us to carry into effect the honest maxims which have distinguished our orderly Government. Now this has not been the case elsewhere; the desolating wars of Napoleon having utterly disorganized most of the European administrations.

very general. Lord Colchester says* in 1820, that England and Denmark "are the only countries which have not confiscated or reduced the sums due to their creditors."

VI.

Holland : THIS wide statement may not be true. I should not have supposed it true of Holland; though the disturbance caused during its long occupation by the French, might well justify national bankruptcy.

its heavy debt, Its debt however, is very heavy, and far exceeds that of any other nation, with the exception of England : as I have shown, it is 23 £ per head of population; against 28 £ in the case of Great Britain, and 14 £ in the case of France.

wonderfully diminished, But it is astonishing to find how much the Dutch have done in reducing the amount. They have not gone about the world propounding new schemes of finance; nor have they boastfully called upon Europe to admire their reso-

---

* Diary III. 110.

lution; they have simply raised a large revenue, and by a frugal administration of affairs, have secured a surplus.

by one-sixth its amount in eleven years. Between 1850 and 1861, they paid off 200 millions of florins, or nearly one-sixth of their debt: or in English money they paid off 17 millions £ in 11 years; leaving 91 millions £ still owing.

Example to Great Britain. Population for population, Great Britain ought to have paid off ten times as much; or 15 millions £ a year; whereas, during the same number of years, between 1855 and 1866, we borrowed as much as we paid off. We pride ourselves on our honest financial management; we hold ourselves up to Europe and America as the example of what free trade will do; we boast of the taxes reduced in 20 years: and we find that our quiet Dutch neighbours have all the while been working at their debt while we have been sleeping, and in the financial race have left us far behind.

How can Holland spare such sums? I may be asked how it is that Holland has spared so large a sum as 1½ millions £ a year, or what in proportion to population would to us be 15 millions £ a-year. I reply by a quotation from M. Block.*

M. Block's explanation: Dutch opulence. "La richesse des Hollandais est devenue proverbiale; et bien qu'on parle maintenant plus souvent des capitaux anglais, il est possible que non-seulement l'aisance individuelle des Néerlandais, mais même la puissance financière *relative* du petit état qui tient les bouches du Rhin dépassent celle des Anglais et de l'empire britannique.

"Dans tous les cas, les Pay-Bas offrent l'exemple

---

* " Puissance Comparée," Gotha, 1862. P. 98.

d'une contrée qui porte avec une facilité—nous dirions volontiers *élégante*—le poids d'une dette immense et de lourds impôts ; c'est que les dépenses de l'état ne sont pas en disproportion avec les recettes des citoyens."

Dutch Budget, 1861. M. Block gives the Budget for 1861. After deducting the sum appropriated to railroads, the proportionate expenditure is about the same as ours. The revenue is very large ; partly in consequence of the singular colonial contribution of far more than 2 millions £. If only our colonies, instead of mulcting us heavily, would contribute 20 millions £ a-year to our revenue ! In that case, we could easily set aside 15 millions £ a-year as a sinking-fund.

Dutch opulence in agriculture. When we remember that the Dutch were formerly the predominant naval power of the world ; that our navigation laws were framed to encourage our marine at their expense, and succeeded in that purpose ; that the carrying trade of the world is now shared with the English and the Americans ; we shall wonder that the opulence M. Block mentions has not ceased, and that the aquatic Holland has not fallen like Tyre and Carthage. The explanation is furnished by a Belgian Professor. M. de Laveleye tells us* that as commerce declined, capital was applied to the promotion of agriculture ; and that as the result, the productiveness of the land is now greater† than that of Belgium, of Lombardy, and of England (even excluding Scotland and Ireland).

Emile de Laveleye. " La Hollande était autrefois, avec Venise, l'état européen qui devait la plus grande part de sa richesse au commerce et la moindre

---

* Emile de Lavaleye, " La Néerlande," 1865. 253.   † *Ibid.* 279.

à l'agriculture. Ce qui permettait au pays de subsister, ce n'était pas la charrue ouvrant à grand effort le sein d'une terre trop humide et sans cesse menacée par les eaux, c'était le navire sillonnant librement les flots de toutes les mers. Un ancien écrivain hollandais, pour dissimuler l'infériorité de sa patrie au point de vue agricole, disait dans ce latin relevé d'antithèses qu'on aimait alors :—

' *Hollandia non floret agricultura, sed agricultura floret in Hollandia.*'*

" Il faut arriver à une époque récente pour voir la disposition des esprits changer à ce sujet : cette époque est celle du déclin, de la chute même de la république des Provinces-Unies. Elle, qui avait vaincu l'Espagne et glorieusement résisté à la France et à l'Angleterre coalisées, succomba lentement, on le sait, sous les mortelles atteintes d'une guerre de tarifs. Les droits différentiels et l'acte de navigation repoussèrent ses navires de tous les ports ; son commerce fût anéanti, sa marine détruite.   *   *   *

" Il en est des nations comme des hommes. Le sort leur a-t-il été contraire, ont-elles succombé dans une lutte inégale, leur commerce, leur industrie, ont-ils décliné sous l'empire de circonstances adverses, il est encore à leur disposition une source inépuisable de profits et de bien-être qui compensera toutes leurs pertes, qui guérira leurs blessures, et que ne pourront jamais tarir les hasards de la guerre ou les vicissitudes des traités : c'est la terre mise en valeur et toujours prête à récompenser au décuple† tous les sacrifices intelligents qu'on consent à lui faire ; en un mot, c'est l'agriculture. C'est elle en effet qui a soutenu

---

* It is amusing to find the same quotation in M. Horn's recent work, " L'Économie Politique avant les Physiocrates."

† This tenfold promise is, I fear, more declamatory than exact : tenfold the seed perhaps : but what about remuneration for capital and labour ?

autrefois la Lombardie et la Belgique, asservies à l'étranger et privées de leurs anciennes industries, et c'est elle aussi qui, plus récemment, a relevé la Hollande déchue de son antique grandeur commerciale."

General progress in Holland. The English, at present, do not understand the progress that Holland has made : if they could be got to read something less ephemeral than a newspaper, they might become less ignorant of the condition of Europe.

* " Since 1848 not a year has passed without bringing to Holland some new good law or wise alteration of an old one. The provincial and commercial legislation was presently remodelled according to the spirit of the constitution, and the antiquated state of things in which old Dutch, French Imperial, and post-revolutionary Dutch arrangements struggled for the mastery, was superseded by a system instinct with the modern spirit. Trade soon felt the benefit of the new impulse. The navigation laws fell in 1850, and improvements were rapidly made in taxation and the tariff, railways were pushed forward, a geological survey of the whole country was made, and the judicial system was reorganized." . . . .

" We have said enough to show that, since the great change of 1848, Holland has been adopting one after another all those steps which have made the glory of our own legislation during the last five-and-thirty years. In some of these reforms she has followed in our wake; but there are two departments of national life in which, thanks not least to Thorbecke, she is far in advance of ourselves, as of

---

* Grant Duff, 296.

145

every other European nation. These are—1. Her ecclesiastical system : and 2. Her elementary education."

Holland concluded. Holland then, is an opulent, frugal, progressive country, with a heavy debt, fast diminishing, the interest on which is paid without the least difficulty.

VII.

Recapitulation of foreign countries. WE find on the whole, that foreign countries may teach us some lessons.

United States. The Americans, I fear, will not set us that example of which they gave promise. They possess, at any rate in the North, a fourth-of-July patriotism, which, being universally diffused and annually blown into a flame, secures an unanimity and constancy of action whenever the Union is in danger : but which may not perhaps prove strong enough to maintain such taxation as will be annually required for the budget, and to carry out a considerable sinking-fund. They may end with awaiting the progress of population to lessen the burden as it has in our case. They may recollect that in seventy years their numbers augmented eight-fold;* that is, about doubled every 23 years on the average : they have still to see how much this rate of progress will be reduced by their future heavy taxation.

France. The French compared with us, have been an imprudent people. Starting after 1815

---

* From 1790 to 1860, 4 millions became 32.

U

with little debt, they have incurred a very heavy one, while we have slightly reduced ours. Revolutions have cost them dear, by preventing any care for futurity. No doubt, they can bear their present taxation without difficulty: but their weight in Europe, great as it is, would be far more formidable, if the frugal maxims of the first Napoleon had guided the administration.

Examples for imitation. But if the United States and France teach us the dangers of profusion, other countries set us better examples for imitation.

Sweden and Prussia. It is too late for us now to follow in the wake of Sweden, which owes but little, and even that little it is said for productive outlay on railroads :* we have our debt and we must deal with it as we can. Norway also, and the greater country Prussia, may move our envy by their freedom from heavy debt ; and as we cannot arrive at this exemption, we must comfort ourselves with the reflection that our superior productiveness enables us now to easily bear our load.

Holland. From Holland we really ought to learn a valuable lesson. That small country has reduced its debt steadily at the rate of a million and a half sterling a-year ; while we, with something like equal opulence and ten times the population, have not reduced ours at all since 1855.

No doubt, the Dutch derive a large income from their colonies. On the other hand, they have lost their ancient maritime predominance, and have maintained their opulence only by diverting their capital to the improvement of agriculture. They do not possess those vast and varied manufactures, which during the last hundred years have caused the

---

* See *Times*, 22 Aug., 1861, and *Economist*, 1059, p. 1383.

prosperity of Great Britain. They equal or surpass us in wealth, principally because they are individually more frugal : we should be compelled to imitate them a little if a tax were imposed for the especial purpose of supporting a sinking-fund.

CHAPTER V.

OUR PRESENT DUTY.

I.

Recapitulation. IN the four previous chapters, I have recalled such facts as I have thought useful for answering the question: what ought we to do?

I have inquired what is the easiest course for an individual who has an estate burdened with debt; and I have shown that a prompt sacrifice is his true policy, because it enlists time and compound interest on his side.

I have given a short history of the different sinking-funds of Great Britain; and especially of those of 1716 and 1786.

I have offered an Indian illustration, for the purpose of solving the problems that presented themselves in the two first chapters; and I have then carefully inquired why the sinking-fund of 1786 broke down, though established at first on a solid basis. I have concluded that in trying to carry it on during a long war, too much was attempted; and that if in 1793 the sinking-fund had been entirely suspended, it might have come into operation again soon after the Peace of 1815, and might since that time have performed good service.

I have given a sketch of the progress of debt and of repayment, in the principal European countries, and in the United States: arriving at this conclusion; that as we cannot follow Prussia and Sweden in their freedom from debt, we ought to gravely consider whether Holland does not supply us with a worthy example of prudence and honesty.

II.

Division into three parts: the heads. I WILL divide this chapter into three parts, under the following heads:—

1. Are the evils of a national debt as great as they are imagined to be?
2. Are there in this country any circumstances tending to mitigate or aggravate those evils?
3. Would a systematic Sinking-Fund correct those evils?

III.

PART I.

Are the evils of a National Debt as great as they are imagined to be?

D. Hume's opinions. I AM dealing here, not with the payment of debt but with the debt itself; and as to this first question, it is well to remove ourselves from our present position, and to recollect what has been thought of national debt by the great writers of a former day. What said David Hume a hundred years ago, when the debt was comparatively small?

Greatness of British efforts. It is interesting to see that in the first half of the last century, the English energy and national resolution to conquer at whatever cost, were displayed just as much as afterwards in the wars of the French revolution.*

" But† what expedient can the public now employ even supposing trade to continue in the most flourishing condition, in order to support its foreign wars and enterprises, and to defend its own honour and interest, or those of its allies ? I do not ask how the public is to exert *such a prodigious power* as it has maintained during our late wars ; where we have so much exceeded, not only our own natural strength, but even *that of the greatest empires.* This extravagance is the abuse complained of, as the source of all the dangers to which we are at present exposed."

Supineness as to financial danger. There was also the same present carelessness as to the future.

‡ " I must confess that there has a strange supineness, from long custom, creeped into all ranks of men, with regard to public debts, not unlike what divines so vehemently complain of with regard to their religious doctrines. We all own that the most sanguine imagination cannot hope, either that this or any future ministry will be possessed of such rigid and steady frugality, as to make a considerable progress in the payment of our debts ; or that the situation of foreign affairs will, for any long time, allow them leisure and tranquillity for such an undertaking. *What then is to become of us?* Were we ever so good Christians, and ever so

---

* I fear it is only of late that we can pretend to have followed the first part of the sound advice of Polonius :—
" . . . Beware
Of *entrance* to a quarrel : but, being in,
Bear it that the opposer may beware of thee."

† Hume, Essay on Public Credit, Ed. 1825. 1, 355.   ‡ *Ib.* 357.

resigned to Providence; this, methinks, were a curious question, even considered as a speculative one, and what it might not be altogether impossible to form some conjectural solution of."

<small>National languor; perhaps bankruptcy,</small> Hume feared a reaction after these violent and extravagant national efforts. * "We have always found, where a government has mortgaged all its revenues, that it necessarily sinks into a state of languor, inactivity, and impotence." Bankruptcy might follow; though he rather hoped than believed that it would. † "So great dupes are the generality of mankind, that, notwithstanding such a violent shock to public credit, as a voluntary bankruptcy in England would occasion, it would not probably be long ere credit would again revive in as flourishing a condition as before." . . "Our popular government, perhaps, will render it difficult or dangerous for a minister to venture on so desperate an expedient as that of a voluntary bankruptcy. And though the House of Lords be altogether composed of proprietors of land, and the House of Commons chiefly; and consequently neither of them can be supposed to have great property in the funds: yet the connexions of the members may be so great with the proprietors, as to render them more tenacious of public faith *than prudence, policy, or even justice, strictly speaking, requires."*

<small>under the pressure of necessity.</small> "But‡ it is more probable, that the breach of national faith will be the necessary effect of wars, defeats, misfortunes, and public calamities, or even perhaps of victories and conquests. I must confess, when I see Princes and States fighting and quarrelling, amidst their

---

* Essay on Public Credit, Ed. 1825. 1, 357. † Ib. 359 and 361. ‡ Ib. 358.

debts, funds, and public mortgages, it always brings to my mind a match of cudgel-playing fought in a China shop. How can it be expected, that Sovereigns will spare a species of property, which is pernicious to themselves and to the public, when they have so little compassion on lives and properties, that are useful to both? Let the time come (and surely it will come) when the new funds, created for the exigencies of the year, are not subscribed to, and raise not the money projected. Suppose either that the cash of the nation is exhausted; or that our faith, which has hitherto been so ample, begins to fail us. Suppose that, in this distress, the nation is threatened with an invasion; a rebellion is suspected or broken out at home; a squadron cannot be equipped for want of pay, victuals, or repairs; or even a foreign subsidy cannot be advanced. What must a prince or minister do in such an emergence? The right of self-preservation is unalienable in every individual, much more in every community. And the folly of our Statesmen must then be greater than the folly of those who first contracted debt, or, what is more, than that of those who trusted, or continue to trust this security, if these Statesmen have the means of safety in their hands, and do not employ them. The funds,* created and mortgaged, will by that time bring in a large yearly revenue, sufficient for the defence and security of the nation : Money is perhaps lying in the exchequer, ready for the discharge of the quarterly interest : necessity calls, fear urges, reason exhorts, compassion alone exclaims : The money will immediately be seized for the current service, under

---

* That is, taxes imposed and money borrowed on the security of those particular taxes, as was the practice even till the present century. The word "funds" meant at first the taxes pledged : it meant afterwards the money borrowed on that security.

the most solemn protestations, perhaps, of being immediately replaced. But no more is requisite. The whole fabric, already tottering, falls to the ground, and buries thousands in its ruins. And this, I think, may be called the *natural death* of public credit; for to this period it tends as naturally as an animal body to its dissolution and destruction."

One of two events must happen: "either* the nation must destroy public credit, or public credit will destroy the nation. It is impossible that they can both subsist, after the manner they have been hitherto managed, in this, as well as in some other countries."

Hume missed one important element. Hume did not appreciate one important element: he failed to make due allowance for the fact, that governments have strong reasons of self-interest for regularity in paying the dividends on their debts. The unfailing punctuality of England is a leading cause of the low rate at which it can borrow: Russia, following the same wise policy, commands terms far more favourable than might be expected in the case of a half-eastern country, only as yet struggling into civilization: Spain, carelessly pursuing the contrary course, is excluded from the bourses of Europe, until it learns that national honesty is the best policy: even the United States, though the Central Government has formerly distinguished itself by discharging principal as well as interest, has shared the discredit caused by Sydney Smith's "drab-coated men of Pennsylvania." The vast enlargement of national debts during a century, has taught governments by experience, the lessons lisped by Addison's "Spectator" on national credit.

---

* *Ibid*, 357.

Hume's failure in prophecy, It must be confessed then, that Hume's prophecies have been unfulfilled: that he was too positive in his predictions and too confident in his power of foretelling the future.

"These* seem to be the events, which are not very remote, and which reason foresees as clearly almost as she can do anything that is in the womb of time. And though the ancients maintained that, in order to reach the gift of prophecy, a certain divine fury or madness was requisite, one may safely affirm that, in order to deliver such prophecies as these, no more is necessary than merely to be in one's senses, free from the influence of popular madness and delusion."

far less than it appears. On the other hand, if he had guarded himself by only pointing out tendencies, and conceding that in any one country, those tendencies might be counteracted by peculiar circumstances, he would have avoided the imputation of rash prophecy: for as I have already shown, on the high authority of Lord Colchester,† things turned out in nearly every instance as Hume anticipated: England and Denmark having been the only two countries, up to 1820, which had unfailingly met their engagements.

IV.

Adam Smith: concedes some advantage, ADAM Smith's "Wealth of Nations" was written later than Hume's Essay; and when the national debt had grown to about‡ 130 millions £., with an annual

---

* *Ibid*, 362. † Diary III, 110.
‡ A. Smith. Book V. Chap. 3. Pa. 419, 420. Ed. 1839.

taxation of about 10 millions £. Though Adam Smith condemns the practice of borrowing generally, he does not deny that it sometimes has its advantages.

"As* in this case, however, the taxes are lighter than they would have been, had a revenue sufficient for defraying the same expense been raised within the year, the private revenue of individuals is necessarily less burdened, and consequently their ability to save and accumulate some part of that revenue into capital is a good deal less impaired. If the method of funding destroy more old capital, it at the same time hinders less the accumulation or acquisition of new capital than that of defraying the public expense by a revenue raised within the year. Under the system of funding, the frugality and industry of private people can more easily repair the breaches which the waste and extravagance of government may occasionally make in the general capital of the society."

but pronounces on the whole ruinous. On the whole however, Adam Smith follows his friend in regarding the system as fatal. If Hume says† that the abuses of national mortgaging are certain, and inevitably lead to " poverty, impotence, and subjection to foreign powers ; " and that ‡ " the practice appears ruinous beyond all controversy ; " Smith also speaks § of " the ruinous expedient of perpetual funding."

Promotes war. He shows how it leads to unnecessary war, by facilitating the acquisition of the necessary means. When governments, he says,‖ want to go to war, they hesitate to levy additional taxes, fearing to disgust the people: but " borrowing delivers them from the embarrassment which this fear and inability

---
* *Ibid*, 420. Col. 1.
† Pa. 348.   ‡ Pa. 347.   § Pa. 418. 2.   ‖ Pa. 417. 2.

would otherwise occasion. By means of borrowing they are enabled, with a very moderate increase of taxes, to raise from year to year money sufficient for carrying on the war; and by the practice of perpetual funding, they are enabled, with the smallest possible increase of taxes, to raise annually the largest possible sum of money." There is another evil. "In great empires, the people who live in the capital, and in the provinces remote from the scene of action, feel, many of them, scarce any inconveniency from the war, but enjoy at their ease the amusement of reading in the newspapers the exploits of their own fleets and armies. To them this amusement compensates the small difference between the taxes which they pay on account of the war and those which they had been accustomed to pay in time of peace. They are commonly dissatisfied with the return of peace, which puts an end to this amusement, and to a thousand visionary hopes of conquest and national glory, from a longer continuance of the war."

Loans fall on capital. Again; taxes generally fall on the expenditure of the people. * "When, for defraying the expenses of government, a revenue is raised within the year from the produce of free or unmortgaged taxes, a certain portion of the revenue of private people is only turned away from maintaining one species of unproductive labour towards maintaining another." But when money is borrowed it is taken from those savings, which would otherwise have been applied as capital to the promotion of production.

Experience. Experience has proved how bad are the actual consequences. † "The practice of fund-

---

* Pa. 420. † Pa. 422. 2.

ing has gradually enfeebled every state which has adopted it. The Italian republics seem to have begun it. Genoa and Venice, the only two remaining which can pretend to an independent existence, have both been enfeebled by it. Spain seems to have learned the practice* from the Italian republics, and (its taxes being probably less judicious than theirs) it has, in proportion to its natural strength, been still more enfeebled. The debts of Spain are of very old standing. It was deeply in debt before the end of the sixteenth century, about a hundred years before England owed a shilling. France, notwithstanding all its natural resources, languishes under an oppressive load of the same kind. The republic of the United Provinces is as much enfeebled by its debts as either Genoa or Venice. Is it likely that in Great Britain alone a practice which has brought either weakness or desolation into every other country should prove altogether innocent?"

V.

Hume and Blackstone: funds are not wealth.

HUME and Smith were rash in uttering their prophecies of certain ruin. They were right however, in exposing the popular fallacies. Men were found at that time, as men have been found since, who deemed a national debt an addition to the wealth of the country.

† "What, then, shall we say to the new paradox, that public encumbrances are, of themselves, advantageous, independent of the necessity of con-

---

* Meaning not the practice of borrowing but of funding.
† Hume 1. 348.

tracting them; and that any state, even though it were not pressed by a foreign enemy, could not possibly have embraced a wiser expedient for promoting commerce and riches, than to create funds, and debts, and taxes, without limitation? Reasonings such as these, might naturally have passed for trials of wit among rhetoricians, like the panegyrics on folly and a fever, on Busiris and Nero, had we not seen such absurd maxims patronized by great ministers, and by a whole party among us."

Blackstone. Mr. McCulloch quotes from Blackstone, the following reply to this paradox.*

" By means of our national debt, the quantity of property in the kingdom is greatly increased in idea, compared with former times; yet, if we coolly consider it, not at all increased in reality. We may boast of large fortunes, and quantities of money in the funds. But where does this money exist? It exists only in name, in paper, in public faith, in parliamentary security: and that is undoubtedly sufficient for the creditors of the public to rely on. But then, what is the pledge which the public faith has pawned for the security of those debts? The land, the trade, and the personal industry of the subject; from which the money must arise that supplies the several taxes. In these, therefore, and in these only, the property of the public creditors does really and intrinsically exist: and of course the land, the trade, and the personal industry of individuals, are diminished in their true value just so much as they are pledged to answer. If A's income amount to £100 per annum, and he is so far indebted to B that he pays him £50 per annum for his interest, one-half of the value of A's property is transferred to B the creditor. The

---

* McCulloch's "Adam Smith," 421 note.

creditor's property exists in the demand which he has upon the debtor, and nowhere else; and the debtor is only a trustee to his creditor for one-half of the value of his income. In short, the property of a creditor of the public consists in a certain portion of the national taxes : by how much, therefore, he is the richer, by so much the nation, which pays these taxes, is the poorer. Commentaries, vol. 1, p. 327."

Payment of right hand to left: Adam Smith: Adam Smith protests against another fallacy. "In* the payment of the interest of the public debt, it has been said, it is the right hand which pays the left. The money does not go out of the country. It is only a part of the revenue of one set of the inhabitants which is transferred to another, and the nation is not a farthing the poorer."

He says afterwards:—†" To transfer from the owners of those two great sources of revenue, land and capital stock, from the persons immediately interested in the good condition of every particular portion of land, and in the good management of every particular portion of capital stock, to another set of persons, (the creditors of the public, who have no such particular interest,) the greater part of the revenue arising from either, must in the long run, occasion both the neglect of land, and the waste or removal of capital stock. A creditor of the public has, no doubt, a general interest in the prosperity of the agriculture, manufactures, and commerce of the country, and consequently, in the good condition of its lands, and in the good management of its capital stock. Should there be any general failure or declension in any of these things, the produce of the different taxes might no longer be sufficient to

---

* Book V. Chap. 3., pa. 421. See also Hume, 352.
† A. Smith, 422.

pay him the annuity or interest which is due to him. But a creditor of the public, considered merely as such, has no interest in the good condition of any particular portion of land, or in the good management of any particular portion of capital stock: as a creditor of the public he has no knowledge of any such particular portion—he has no inspection of it — he can have no care about it. Its ruin may in some cases be unknown to him, and cannot directly affect him."

<small>might be carried a step further.</small> May not this argument be carried a step further? Adam Smith mentions land and capital, the sources of rent and profit: ought he to omit labour, the source of wages? It appears to me that the national debt is a great evil, not only because it necessitates taxes on landlords and on capitalists, but also because it necessitates them on labourers. We have to take a part of the earnings of the ploughman and of the artisan, and to hand it to the owner of Consols. It is an evil that tea and sugar, and even that beer, should be enhanced in price. Adam Smith seems to have believed that a rise in the cost of living caused an equivalent rise in wages; and that thus the labourer recouped himself for any tax on his subsistence. But if he had seen, as we have, the very varying rates of wages, even where paid by the piece, in one age and another, in one country and another, and even in one occupation and another, he would probably have modified his opinion; and would therefore have added to the list of evils, that of raising the prices of commodities and thus diminishing the enjoyments of the labourers.

VI.

Dr. Price's views: THESE great writers treated the subject as statesmen: Dr. Price treated it as an actuary. He pointed out that when a sum of money was levied by taxation, it was paid once for all; but that when it was borrowed, there was interest to be paid on it for a year, for 14 years, for 100 years, for ever; and that consequently, for every million borrowed there was repaid, 2, 10, or 100 millions.

Russian illustration: Let us take an individual case. Mr. Grant Duff tells us[*] that we are deceived as to the opulence of Russian noblemen, by the fact, that "many Russians of moderate means appear very rich when they travel, because they are spending their capital."

Nobleman saves and then spends. Say that one of "the 120 Prince Galitzins"[†] resolves to spend in this way 10,000 £ beyond his ordinary revenue. If he is prudent he will save this sum in previous years: in that case, he lays out on European travel, what would otherwise have gone for everyday pleasures, or for visits to the capital. This is like a tax levied on the ordinary expenditure of a people: the payers have lost a certain amount of gratification, and they have received their share of national protection or assistance.

Borrows: repays twice or more. But it is probable that the 10,000 £ would be borrowed. If the interest be 5 per cent., the nobleman has to pay 500 £ a year in future: at the end of 20 years, he will have paid 10,000 £ for interest; that is, he will

---

[*] "Studies in European Politics," 113.   [†] *Ibid.* 113.

have paid the very amount he borrowed, and will still owe his 10,000 £. Thus it is, says Price, with a national debt: every 30 years we repay what we borrowed, and still we owe the same amount. A million that we borrowed in 1688, has now been paid six, eight, or ten times over.

If at compound interest. Price and his school, however, like to represent everything in the light of compound interest. Suppose that the Russian, on his return home, fails to diminish his ordinary expenditure; and therefore, has to borrow again each year, in order to pay the interest due. Here, it will not take 20 years to make him vainly pay the 10,000 £ he borrowed : 14 years at 5 per cent. compound interest will do it ; and if he continues this ruinous practice 28 years, he will have paid 30,000 £, and will still owe the original sum. But this is just what most European nations have done : they have had a debt constantly increasing ; that is under one excuse or another, they have borrowed the money with which they have met the interest due on loans. Although in time of peace the English nation has generally avoided borrowing, yet its debt has increased from a million in 1689, to 13 millions in 1702, to 36 millions in 1714, to 133 millions in 1763, to nearly 250 millions in 1784, to 840 millions in 1817. Since 1817 we have paid that unfortunate 840 millions nearly twice over in the form of interest, and yet we still owe 800 millions : and if we were to reckon what our payments would amount to if we had invested the same sums at compound interest, it might go near to the present value of all our properties real and personal.

VII.

Great Britain not ruined, AFTER all, Great Britain is not ruined; she is not enfeebled; she has not sunk into a condition of languor; she is not cursed with impotence: on the contrary; she is stronger than ever; her taxation is not intolerable; her national resources appear unbounded; her agriculture is productive; her manufactures flourish; her commerce covers the globe. If it is not material prosperity that we lack, but as I fear, a proportionate moral and intellectual improvement, that does not detract from our abundant political good fortune.

but heavily burdened. 1815, &c. But though we are not ruined; though the steam engine and the cotton trade and the hardware manufactures, have saved us from the fate predicted by philosophers; yet we have had a narrow escape from the ill-fortune that has befallen other nations. During the seven years that followed the peace of 1815, there were manufacturing and commercial uneasiness, political disaffection, and an unfailing cry of agricultural distress. The income-tax had been indignantly cast off with the war; but the necessaries of life were taxed, and superfluities and luxuries were heavily taxed.

1825, &c. Gradually, trade revived; until in 1825 there came the crisis of one of our decennial follies. In 1835 there was another commercial blood-letting; and from that time till 1842 the resources of the nation seem to have lost their elasticity, and the successive Chancellors of the Exchequer found a difficulty in raising the necessary taxes.

1842, &c. In 1842, Sir R. Peel reimposed the income-tax, as a necessary means towards remitting other taxes, and thus restoring the spring of the public resources. The Irish famine completed our free trade policy, the success of which is undisputed, and is being gradually imitated by all the great European nations.

Now: Since those financial changes, commerce has prospered, our manufactures have grown, our exports have tripled. Tax upon tax has been remitted, and yet the exchequer is full : sixty to seventy millions are raised more easily than eight or ten millions a century ago.

the evil continues great. Nevertheless, the National Debt is a great evil ; for it requires an annual taxation of 24 to 25 millions £ : * this heavy charge prevents us from remitting the duties on tea and sugar ; it makes us grudge the expenditure on our fleet, which is absolutely necessary now that the bread we eat may be cut off by an enemy at sea ; it restrains us from heartily promoting the education of the people, and limits our assistance to a poor three-quarters of a million £, while as compared with the Americans we ought to spend 7 or 8 millions £.

McCulloch's apology Mr. McCulloch indeed, in the spirit of an optimist, apologised for loans, and went so far as almost to say that they had added to the national capital; and that the taxes raised to pay the interest stimulated industry and invention, and thus perhaps enriched the people.

† " It has been doubted by some whether the existing capital of the country would have been really greater than it is, had the late war not occurred. It is difficult to come to an exact conclusion upon such

---

* The debt is about 800 millions ; at 3 per cent. the interest would be 24 millions ; the charges for management have to be added. Besides, we pay more than a million additional for terminable annuities, which excess constitutes a sinking-fund.

† McCulloch's " Adam Smith," 1839. 153 note.

a point, but we are very far from supposing, had there been no war, that all, or even the greater part of the vast sums expended in carrying it on, would have been added to the national capital. The gradually increasing pressure of taxation stimulated the industrious portion of the community to make corresponding efforts to preserve their place in society; and gave a spur to industry and invention, and produced a spirit of economy that we should in vain have attempted to excite by any less powerful means. Had taxation been very oppressive, it would not have had this effect; but it was not so high as to produce dejection or despair; though it was at the same time sufficiently heavy to render a considerable increase of exertion and parsimony necessary to prevent it from encroaching on the fortunes of individuals, or at all events from diminishing the rate at which they had previously been increasing." Referring afterwards to this note, he says,*

" Neither must the indirect effect of loans, and of the taxes imposed to defray the interest, be lost sight of. When these taxes are not carried to too great a height, they exert a very beneficial influence over industry, and go far, by the stimulus they give to invention and economy, to replace, and sometimes more than replace, the sums lent to Government."

ill-founded. I agree with those who hold that it is sometimes necessary for a nation to make heavy pecuniary sacrifices for a great object: no patriotic Dutchman can regret the outlay incurred and the debt accumulated, first in freeing his nation from the fanatical zeal of Philip II., and afterwards in protecting it from the wanton attacks of Louis XIV. :

* *Ib.* 421, note.

nor do I much complain that my own country was
dragged into the vortex of the French revolution,
and emerged with reputation undamaged, but with
the largest debt the world had seen.

Mr. McCulloch's apology for debt and taxation
however, seems to me worthy to rank with the
paradox ridiculed by Hume, as belonging to those
" reasonings " which " might naturally have passed
for trials of wit among rhetoricians, like the panegyrics on folly and a fever, on Busiris and Nero."

Mr. McCulloch says that the war taxes were not
very oppressive : he seems to have forgotten that all
persons of fixed incomes were cruelly oppressed by
them, to the extent in many cases of having had to
give up housekeeping and to retire into lodgings ;
and anyone may see the same distress in the corresponding class among the Americans now : he
seems also to have forgotten that the earlier years
of the war ground down the labouring classes, and
particularly in the rural districts, in a way unexampled in this country ; a result partly owing to bad
harvests, but more to the difficulty of importing
food and the general rise in prices caused by the
war.

Evils only partly counter-balanced. It is easy to say that certain good effects followed in the form of industry and frugality : this is only an example of
the trite rule that there is a " soul of good in things
evil." " Sweet are the uses of adversity :" but we
are not therefore, to say that adversity is prosperity,
or that national adversity is on the whole as desirable
as national prosperity. And as to taxation : we find
Prussia* a few years ago, levying just half the sum
per head that we levied ; does any sane man pity

---

* M. Block, " Puissance Comparée," 159.

Prussia on that account? Would any Statesman, deliberately adopting Mr. McCulloch's principle, double the taxation of his country, not for the sake of the money thus raised, but in order to stimulate industry, and strengthen frugality?

CONCLUSION OF PART I.

I conclude that the evil of a national debt is very great : that if the predictions made by Hume and Adam Smith have not been fulfilled in the case of Great Britain, yet they have been fulfilled in the case of most other countries : that as Dr. Price pointed out, a nation which borrows, pays its whole debt over and over again in periods of 20 or 30 years, even if we suppose only simple interest ; and in still shorter periods if we suppose compound interest: that therefore, loans ought not to be resorted to unless under the pressure of extreme necessity.

VIII.

PART II.

Are there in this country any circumstances tending to aggravate or mitigate the evils?

Our own case discussed. GRANTING then, that a National Debt does cause great evils in many ways, and especially by compelling repayment over and over again in the form of interest, let us inquire whether our own circumstances are such as to cause mitigation or aggravation.

Some say, money spent is irrecoverably gone. The money has been spent, say some writers: the country is to that extent the poorer: you cannot cancel the expenditure and recal the capital wasted. Leave things alone now and let the debt continue as a memento for the future. Such persons assume that our present condition is a permanent one; and that no future wars, convulsions of nature, or commercial disasters, will weaken our actual strength: they assume that because for the present we meet our engagements with tolerable ease, therefore, we need not anticipate future difficulty.

Our credit is really high enough. I concede that some former reasons for reducing our debt, have almost ceased to exist. At several periods of our history, a large addition to the debt had weakened the credit of the government, and the high rate at which further loans have had to be contracted, has made it imperative to reduce the amount of the debt. The very low rate at which the British government now borrows, exhibits a strength of credit that wants no support. In 1862, M. Block* gave the following as the rates at which European nations could borrow:—10 per cent., Turkey; 6 to 7 per cent., Italy, Portugal, Austria, and Spain; 5 per cent., Russia; over 4, and under 5 per cent., France, Sweden, and Prussia; 4 per cent., Holland; something over $3\frac{3}{4}$ per cent., Belgium and Denmark; $3\frac{1}{4}$ per cent., Great Britain only. Considerable changes have since taken place: Russia cannot borrow at 5 per cent.; much less can Italy borrow under 7 per cent. Even the English rate is not quite so low as it once was; but this is accounted for by a general rise in the rate of interest; a fact

---

* " Puissance Comparée, Gotha," 1862. 166.

which is notorious, but of which I may offer as a proof, that the great insurance company, The Scottish Widows' Fund Society, got 4½ per cent. on their investments in 1866, against 4 per cent. in 1860.

It appears therefore, that the credit of the British government is higher than that of any other government; and that it is not on the ground of facilitating future loans, that the necessity of a sinking-fund can be founded.

Taxation not intolerable. Again, it cannot be maintained that our taxation is unusually oppressive. Very heavy it certainly is, and few people share Mr. McCulloch's optimism in speaking lightly of the burden : but population and wealth considered, it is light as compared with what it was in 1815 ; our English population having since that date about doubled, and our means of paying taxes having perhaps trebled, in the three kingdoms taken together, while the peace taxes have not increased by one-half, and are probably not half so oppressive as they were fifty years ago. Great complaints are made indeed, of the recent increase of national expenditure, which from 50 millions has run up to 65 : this is certainly a matter of great regret. But it must be carefully recollected that our account of expenditure now includes nearly 5 millions for the cost of collection, which it did not formerly : the expenditure also was not precisely 50 millions, but in 1848-9, 53 millions ; in 1853-4, 51 millions.* We may say on the whole, that we have increased our expenditure 10 millions in the last 14 years ; an alarming augmentation I confess. Unfortunately, there seems little hope of our returning to the lower scale, because we have only done what other great

---

* Northcote, 382, 387.

nations have done to a far greater extent. We are told that between 1828 and 1861, the taxes have increased in European countries at the following rates :—* from 100 : in Russia to 446 ; in Spain to 376 ; in Austria to 288 ; in Prussia to 266 ; in Holland to 158 ; in France to 176 ; in Belgium to 152 ; in Great Britain to only 133 : that is, that they have increased four-fold in Russia, and only by one-third in Great Britain ; or, that for every 3£ paid before, we pay 4£ and Russia 12£. If a general disarmament were possible, we might perhaps get back towards our old 50 millions £ of taxation ; for though we now wisely spend a considerable sum on education and the promotion of art, we pay far less than formerly for interest on the debt.

After all, I cannot say that the taxation of England is so oppressive as to call for any unusual measures for the reduction of interest on the debt : the free trade policy of the last twenty years has conferred on the nation a rejuvenescence that enables it to bear its load with alacrity.

It would be unreasonable therefore, to advocate the establishment of a sinking-fund, in order to strengthen the national credit.

IX.

Possible disadvantages of repayment: Hamilton, Grenville.

IT is alleged by objectors, not merely that a sinking-fund brings no advantage, but even that it may be positively mischievous : that it acts on the public as a narcotic: for, says Hamilton,† "The confidence

---

* Block, " Puissance Comparée," 1862, 159.
† Inquiry, 1813, pa. 5.

placed in the efficacy of these schemes has contributed further to ease the alarm which the magnitude of the public debt would otherwise have produced;" and Lord Grenville says,* "To reduce debt by borrowing to the same amount on terms of equal or greater disadvantage, is a manifest fiction in finance; —a fiction in that branch of government, in which, above all others, fiction is most to be condemned. Its mischief is nothing less than this; it disguises from the country, and, in some degree, from the government, and from Parliament itself, the real state of some of our most important interests; throwing over them a false colour of progressive improvement in the very moments when the public debt is most rapidly increasing, and when the public revenue has become most unequal to its charge."

Possibility conceded. Both these objections apply to a sinking-fund such as once existed, but not to such a one as might be established. Lord Grenville indeed, in his disgust at the failure of Pitt's scheme, which he had himself helped to establish, went the length of condemning all sinking-funds: Hamilton, at an earlier period, while war was still raging, was more moderate; contenting himself with showing the losses caused by the particular scheme, but acknowledging that notwithstanding its faults, it had led to an increase of taxation, which had really restrained the growth of the debt. Hamilton showed clearly, that the nation would have been better off, if instead of applying that additional taxation to extinguishing debt, it had applied it directly to the expenses of government, and had therefore borrowed less: if it had prevented the necessity of debt, instead of first incurring it,

---

* Essay, 1828, pa. 11.

and then discharging it. On the whole, Hamilton was of opinion that Pitt's sinking-fund had done good by leading to increased taxation; but that the increased taxation might have been better applied. It is quite conceivable however, that a sinking-fund might do positive mischief; by the expense of its machinery, and by the creation of a false public confidence, without leading to increased taxation.

Particularly, if bad taxation: the United States. Again, if a sinking-fund were maintained by pernicious taxes, this evil might outweigh the good proposed. The people of the United States showed an earnest desire at the close of the civil war, to begin at once an effective reduction of their national debt: a patriotic desire, at a time when they were groaning under heavy and unaccustomed imposts. The *Economist* said however,* in an article on a Taxation Commission :—" The Commission are opposed '*at present*,' to the payment of debt. They consider that the taxes which would be imposed to raise the necessary surplus would cripple the nation, harass production, and make the nation poorer in the end. And in this a European economist would probably agree with them. Very great pruning must be applied to the internal revenue of the United States before it can be expedient to use a surplus accruing from such revenue for an object so secondary as the reduction of a national debt."

Opinion of the Commissioners, Such are the opinions of the Commission and of the *Economist* ; and though I might object to speak of the reduction of the debt as "an object so secondary," yet I quite agree with the reasons assigned for preferring the reduction of oppressive taxation.

---

* *Economist*, 7th April, 1866, p. 407.

and of the Secretary of Treasury. We learn from the *Economist* that a high authority holds a different opinion. "Whether* the Americans have at their disposal enough good taxes for this purpose, a very scrupulous examination and much experience alone can decide. The Secretary of the Treasury, the highest American financial officer, believes that there are such good taxes; and in deference to his known opinion the Commission devote 10,000,000 £ out of their anticipated 27,000,000 £ to the payment of the principal of the debt, which leaves them 17,000,000 £ applicable to the reduction of taxation."

The Commissioners' Report appeared in the Spring of 1866. I have already shown that the condition of the Americans a year later was very unfavourable: that prices were extravagantly high, that the rates of wages and salaries had not risen in the same proportion, and that many kinds of industry were greatly impeded. Then and since, strikes for higher wages have abounded.

Debt not diminished. To crown all, the earnest desire for reduction of debt, is unlikely to be gratified: it has been announced that there will be no reduction in 1867; and we have even been told† that "Mr. M'Culloch‡ has expressed the opinion that it will be necessary temporarily *to increase* the public debt."

Present sinking-fund therefore a mistake in United States. I am quite of opinion that the Americans, under present circumstances, would be utterly wrong, if they tried to levy additional taxation, or even to maintain the present taxation, for the purpose of establishing a sinking-fund of any kind. They might however, do one thing which would enable them to reduce that

---

* *Ibid*, 407. † *Pall Mall Gazette*, May 31, 1867, p. 6.
‡ The American Minister.

part of their taxation which is at present hampering their industry, and seriously reducing its productiveness ; they might practise extreme frugality in every government department. In regard to their military force they certainly behaved admirably : as soon as the war ceased, they disbanded their army with a haste that surprised their European contemporaries ; and we are reminded of the times of Cromwell and his Ironsides, when we hear of an American General becoming a professor in an university, and of a Colonel becoming a railway clerk or a storekeeper. But I cannot see the propriety of the treaty concluded by the President, and confirmed by the Senate, for the purchase of the Russian territory : I sympathize with the indignation of the Lower House, and I should rejoice if they had voided the treaty, as they threatened to do, by refusing to supply the purchase money. In the face of heavy liabilities, and under the smart of present taxation, the people, unless they are greatly changed, will repudiate with indignation all acts which will unnecessarily increase the annual expenditure; and will insist on rigorous frugality in every department of administration.

Conclusion as to bad taxation. In this and in every similar case, it is far more important to readjust taxation, so as to give fair play to all the springs of industry, than it is to establish a sinking-fund, however well contrived. The best of all sinking-funds is an increase of population and opulence : this has reduced our debt virtually to half of what it was : America, since it achieved independence, has increased to eightfold its numbers; and if it could go on at the same rate, it would in the course of another century, reduce the pressure of its debt to one-tenth of what it is now, even if the amount remained unchanged : the danger is, that the pressure of taxation should divert the stream of emigration, and should thus reduce the rate of increase to something nearer that of European countries : from doubling every 23 years, as it did between 1790 and 1860,* to doubling in 52 years as England, in 54 years as Prussia, in 63 years as Sweden, or in 198 years as France.

First, let every nation have judicious taxation, and then a sinking-fund.

X.

Ought England to adopt a system of reduction?
GREAT Britain however, has not pursued a course of bad taxation in order to discharge debt; during the last quarter of a century, taxation has been scientifically re-arranged, while payment of debt has been postponed. Politicians generally are of opinion that the postponement should be continued, and that a systematic reduction of debt is not wanted.

Recapitulation of points I concede.
I concede that reduction is not wanted in order to correct the evils from which our forefathers suffered : that we have no need to facilitate future loans, which can already be obtained with readiness enough : that we are not under the necessity of artificially enhancing the price of Consols, which, if habitually lower than they once or twice have been, still sell at a very high price as compared with that of other securities at home, and with that of the government stocks of other nations : that we cannot hope to force Consols above par, and

---

* *Revue des deux Mondes*, 15th May, 1867, pa. 463. I give the French statement without discussing it.

thus to bring the charge down much below 3 per cent.: that we cannot complain of suffering an intolerable load of taxation, heavy though our imposts are; and that if we could make such a complaint, we should not be relieved from the grievance by a regular sinking-fund, the establishment of which must begin with an increase of taxation.

Analogy of a private person. Nevertheless, I am of opinion that an organized fund ought to be established. In the analogous case of a private person no doubt is felt; a landowner whose estate is burdened with debt, would find every adviser recommending him, and urging him, to save money and discharge his obligations. Let those who maintain a distinction in the case of the nation, show the grounds of their opinion: it certainly rests with them to produce reasons for exonerating the public from the rule, that debts should be paid as soon as possible. On a private estate there is a constant tendency to accumulation of debt; there is the same tendency on the national estate: in both cases there is the same ruinous issue; both landowner and government have to pay the principal over and over again in the form of interest; every twenty or thirty years the sum borrowed is paid back again, and yet the original debt continues undiminished.

XI.

Recapitulation: Hume and Adam Smith. I HAVE shown that two great thinkers of the last century, Adam Smith and Hume, expressed much alarm at the course the British nation was pursuing: that Hume, after speaking of our continental wars as the exertion of a prodigious power, exceeding even that of the greatest empires, expressed a fear that we might afterwards sink into a state of languor, inactivity, and impotence; and more than half hoped for a declaration of insolvency to purge the disorder: that Adam Smith, while he conceded some little advantage to the practice of occasional borrowing, declared it to be on the whole ruinous; appealing to history to prove that France, Venice, Genoa, and Holland, had fallen into weakness or desolation by this means, and asking why Great Britain alone should hope to escape. I have shown also, that according to Lord Colchester, all the European powers except Great Britain and Denmark, had practised repudiation of debt wholly or partially.

Why has Great Britain escaped? Why then, has Great Britain escaped this humiliation? Why has she found the means of meeting her obligations with unfailing punctuality? Certainly not by abandoning the practice of borrowing on perpetual annuities; for it is since Hume and Smith wrote that the bulk of our debt has been incurred: at that time the American Plantations had not revolted, nor had the French Revolution been even predicted: the debt was not a fifth part of what it amounted to in 1815, or of what it amounts to now. Hume and Smith prophesied ruin: the destinies of other nations fulfilled the prediction; but Great Britain went blundering on, wading deeper and deeper into a sea of debt, and to the astonishment of the world escaped perdition.

Not by national honesty alone. Our patriotic sentiments make us willing to believe,-that it is our national honesty which has thus exalted us in the scale of nations. I do not dispute the existence of this admirable sentiment of honesty: I am convinced too

Y

that there is a sturdy and unfailing patriotism*
among the British people, which would be deeply
wounded by any stain on the national escutcheon.
But the most willing horse cannot do the work of
two horses : the most honourable merchant cannot
meet his engagements, if his assets are swallowed up
by an earthquake, or seized by a pasha: Holland
could not perform its natural functions when it was
occupied by the enemy: Great Britain could not
have carried on the French war and also paid 20 to
30 millions £ a year for interest, unless the necessary
taxes had been collected. Whence came the vast
resources that were needed ?

Extension of British manufactures. The phenomenon is capable of a satisfactory explanation: during the closing half of last century, a revolution took place in the economical condition of England. We had been above all things an agricultural people, importing food occasionally when harvests failed, but exporting far more when harvests were good: we became, after Watt and Arkwright, a manufacturing people, importing on the average a considerable proportion of our food. I see it said carelessly, that we kept our food at home because there was a great increase in the mouths to be filled; as though a mere increase of population would prevent the exportation of food: if this were so, how was it that the great increase of population in Ireland did not prevent the exportation of its food? The truth is that we can-

---

* Patriotism is so little appealed to in English life, that we are hardly aware of its existence; but if anyone doubts as to its vitality, let him read the Peninsular Dispatches of the Duke of Wellington, of all men the least addicted to vainglory, but driven by experience to the conviction, that other nations had not in his time the perennial patriotism which he found in England. This is even more true at present, because the correction of abuses, and the kindly exercise of power since 1815, have made us a far more united and patriotic people in Great Britain, if not in Ireland, than we were during the war.

not safely regard a nation as one person, or one family: the food that is produced belongs partly to the labourer as wages, partly to the farmer as profit, partly to the landlord as rent: suppose that the labourers multiply beyond measure, and that the farmers have no employment for the additional hands; as there is nothing to transfer the food from farmer to labourer, and nothing to transfer it from landlord to labourer, the food will be exported as before in spite of the increase of mouths. In England, during the closing half of last century, it was not because there were more mouths to be filled that exportation of food ceased: it was because the capitalists and labourers became able to produce manufactures which landlords and farmers wanted. Landlords and farmers, instead of sending their food to the continent, to be exchanged for goods, sent it to the English manufacturing towns to be so exchanged.

Increase of population, It is true that there was a rapid increase of population. Unfortunately, we have no census of the eighteenth century, the bench of bishops having thrown out a bill for establishing one, just before the interesting era in question. We get scattered notices however. For example, less than a hundred years ago,* Liverpool, Manchester, and Birmingham, taken together, contained only 92,000 persons; in 1801 they had grown to 230,000, exhibiting a rate of increase greater even than that of the present century.

and of wealth as indicated by taxation. The augmentation of wealth must have been rapid during the whole of the eighteenth century, if it were proportionate to the growing productiveness of the taxes.

---

* Statistical Journal, March 1866, pa. 93.

During the war of the Succession in the beginning of Queen Anne's reign, five millions seemed the utmost possible revenue : Adam Smith, sixty years later, speaks with admiration of ten millions : thirty-five to forty years later* we raised about forty-eight millions ; and in the next ten years, sixty-three millions. Notwithstanding the long and costly wars, first with the colonies and then with France, the growth of manufactures and commerce, backed by improved farming, caused such an augmentation of tax-paying power as the world had never dreamt of.

Hume and Smith not complete prophets. Hume and Adam Smith were original thinkers, deeply read in the topics on which they wrote : but they had not the gift of prophecy; they did not foresee that the genius of a few men would invent machines, which eagerly seized upon and developed by their practical and commercial countrymen, would multiply the resources of the nation : they assumed that no such revolution would arise to save us from the consequences of what seemed our financial madness : they thought it self-evident that if a little island, moderately peopled, made efforts worthy of the greatest States, then exhaustion and languor and impotence must follow, as they had followed in the cases of Genoa, Venice, and Holland. Theirs was a case, as it seems to me, of being what is commonly called theoretically right but practically wrong : they were right in their principle, that is in their fundamental law, that reckless funding results in exhaustion, languor, impotence and ruin ; they proved to be wrong in applying that principle to the future of Great Britain, because there were circumstances of

---

* L. Levi, "Taxation," p. 15.

which they were ignorant, that turned out strong enough to triumph over the fatal tendencies they pointed out.

XII.

England's escape, as individuals,
GREAT Britain then, has escaped the doom of headstrong and reckless nations : she has escaped by a wonderful concurrence of events, that no political genius could deliberately prepare, and no human sagacity could predict. Every one who has seen much of commercial affairs, knows that among private persons, and among companies, similar good fortune sometimes falsifies the prophecies of sagacity. An ironmaster bought ground, erected works, sunk coalpits, all without a sufficient capital : insolvency appeared certain ; and if it had come, there would have been a verdict of reckless trading : the sudden extension of railroads caused a brisk demand, prices rose, and a few years' prosperity made this manufacturer's fortune. Many a man dies rich, who, dying at another time, would have been insolvent: many a successful joint stock company has had its years of imminent ruin.

no reason for future escape.
What should we say of the ironmaster, rescued by external circumstances, if he again put his acquired fortune to a similar hazard ? we should pronounce him an idiot. What should we say of the directors who, having narrowly escaped shipwreck, disregarded their experience, and again incurred the same risks ? We should call them either fools or knaves. Unusual good fortune in one instance, is no ground for hoping unusual good

fortune in the future. The same is true of a nation. Our nation has escaped its natural fate of insolvency and ruin : that is no reason for its running the same risks again; no reason for disregarding the lessons taught by the history of others.

Debt indeed, not increased. It may be thought that this is merely an excellent reason for avoiding increase of debt: it may be said that the political world is aware of this; and that our government does not contract debt unless under the pressure of war, or other sudden necessity for expenditure. I do not deny that the British Exchequer is managed with much prudence; nor that the successive ministers have carefully kept the revenue above the expenditure: no difficult task since the adoption of a free trade policy, but yet one which the carelessness of prosperity might have neglected.

XIII.

This is insufficient. THIS avoidance of further debt however, seems to me quite insufficient. We have hitherto enjoyed unmerited prosperity: not only may that cease; we may suffer unmerited misfortune. But disregarding that possibility, we are still bound to act on the ordinary maxim of prudence, that in the days of prosperity we should prepare for adversity. However fair may be the prospects of our immediate future, and even of our future at a little greater distance, we ought to anticipate some period when our commercial greatness will fail. If that failure were imminent, we ought to make immediate and large preparation: if we may hope that it is distant, our preparation ought still to be immediate, but it may safely be moderate. It ought to be immediate; on the principle I have illustrated in my first chapter: in which I have shown that a landholder hampered by debt, may clear his estate with comparative ease by at once setting aside a year's income to accumulate at compound interest; whereas, if he defers that self-denial till the last year of his life, his estate will have but little relief. If we believe that our trade will continue unimpaired for 100 or 120 years, it will be enough for us now to set aside a moderate sum to grow at compound interest.

The future: the next generation, What then, are the prospects of our immediate future? By immediate I do not mean the year or two during which we may still suffer, from the reaction and languor which are following the over-production and wild speculations of the years preceding 1866: I ask what are the prospects of the next generation?

has good prospects. Free trade. I believe that those prospects are bright. In the last century, Great Britain was saved by her manufactures. Afterwards, the long and terrible Napoleonic wars, disturbed our economical condition; and left us with heavy taxation, and still worse, with Corn Laws that hindered our growth. Before 1842, we seemed to be sinking into a stationary and stagnant condition: our exports grew little beyond the regulation 50 millions £; the produce of taxation had ceased to increase. But then, the commercial doctrines of *Boisguillebert* and the *Physiocrates* and Adam Smith, were brought into prominence: Lancashire clamoured for free trade: Peel did what Pitt would fain have done, if the French revolution had not counteracted his resolution to follow the teaching of Adam Smith.

is extending. The amazing success of this movement,

which is quadrupling our exports; which has wiped off all our worst taxes; which without lowering rents, has raised the rate of profit, and has augmented the ordinary rates of wages;* which has benefited alike the individual and the State : the amazing success of this movement in one country, is producing a revolution in the commerce of the world. America at present stands aloof: we shall see whether the intolerable pressure of the burden left by the war, will drive her into wisdom. In Europe, France has been converted to free-trade by the political prudence of her Emperor : the other powers, including Austria and even Russia, are feeling their way. We have done with the "mercantile" system, *mercantilisme*,† or *Colbertisme*, as France calls it : governments are fast learning to carry out Quesnay's maxim of a hundred years ago, *laissez faire, laissez passer*. Commerce therefore, has vast extension before it; and we, as a commercial people, with unlimited and increasing capital, must needs profit. " L'industrie‡ des transports est encore à son enfance dans le monde." France indeed, will share these advantages : she has made an excellent start in the race : so much the better, since there is room for all, and as Adam Smith tells us, the richer the neighbour, the better the customer.

Improved European Agriculture: France. So far our prospects are bright : the extension of steamers and of railroads is also in our favour.. But not only may

---

* We can find political economists who deny that profit and wages can rise at the same time. Ricardo, whose authority is relied on, did, in fact, concede that wages might possibly rise from 10s. to 15s. a week, while profit rose from 10 to 15 per cent.: he only held that if the capitalist took a larger *share* of the whole produce, a smaller *share* would be left for the labourer: an evident but useless truth.

† Horn, " L'Econ. Pol.," &c., pp. 116, 117.

‡ L. de Lavergne, " L'Agriculture," &c., 1865, p. 110.

we look for an augmented facility in exchanging : we may anticipate a greatly increased production in European agriculture, and therefore in commodities to be exchanged. No one pretends that farming has at present reached its maximum productiveness. Of the great European countries, Great Britain is the best farmed : but it is certain that its produce would be greatly multiplied, if all the land were as well managed as that of the Lothians : probably it might be increased by one-half; possibly it might be doubled. There is good cultivation in France, and on a large scale too. La Beauce,* in the department of L'Eure-et-Loire, has large farms, paying a rent of 2 £ to £2 10s. an English acre, with wages at 2s. to 3s. a day, and a yield of wheat of 30 bushels to the acre. This yield indeed, is not very great in one of the ancient granaries of Paris, and in a country of which the soil and climate are superior to ours, if we may trust three authorities, all of whom judged after using their own eyes : I mean Adam Smith, Arthur Young, and Leonce de Lavergne.† La Beauce too, is quite exceptional : it is said that the system of *métayage*, or *bail à moitié fruits*,‡ still prevails throughout a third of France ;§ and this system, though quite consistent with a good condition of the labouring classes, is unfavourable to a large production, because it leads to annual agreements instead of leases, and often to a chronic state of watchful suspicion on the part of the landlord, who fears an unfair division of the produce.|| It appears also that the centre of France, including Auvergne, Périgord, &c., is in a very backward condition.¶

---

* *Economist*, 1201, p. 1028 : and L. de Lavergne, " Écon. Rurale de la France," 1866, p. 111.   † " Écon. Rurale de l'Angleterre," 1863, pp. 1 to 21.
‡ *Ib*. de la France, 314.   § *Revue des deux Mondes*, 69, 614 note.
|| *Ib*., 632, 633, 640.   ¶ L. de Lavergne, " Écon. Rurale de la France," 348.

This stagnant state, we are told, has arisen from the absence of rivers and the want of roads. But the railroads already constructed or in prospect, will correct this evil, and that speedily; because as soon as the market of Paris, or any large provincial town, or any seaport, is open, prices rise rapidly, as happened within my own knowledge in the neighbourhood of Amboise a dozen years ago: this rise stimulates the cultivator, furnishes capital, and immediately increases the produce. The agriculture of France therefore, is likely to multiply its yield.

Russia, and Europe generally. But the backwardness of France is nothing as compared with that of most parts of Europe.

* "Even in Southern Russia, the trifling surplus of grain sold to the west, is raised by wretched farming; the zone which produces it is so vast and of such fertility that it could supply food enough for the whole of Europe, instead of exporting with difficulty four or five millions hectolitres of inferior corn, which often fails through the uncertainty of the seasons.

"Thus, to say nothing of the deserts of Asia, Africa, and America, Europe alone could maintain, with ordinary productiveness, five or six times its present number of inhabitants. Assuming as a maximum the actual condition of Belgium and England, the remainder has long strides to make before overtaking them; Italy and Germany may treble their population, France may double hers, Spain, Portugal, Hungary, Poland, Prussia, may treble theirs, Turkey and Russia may multiply theirs almost tenfold: and assuming, what is true, that Belgium and England may advance still further, a far wider career is open to other nations."

---

* " L. de Lavergne, " L'Agriculture," &c. 1865-72.

Conclusion as to England. Railroads then, with free trade, and a general European tendency to improvement, seem likely to greatly increase production, and in an equal or greater degree to increase exchanges. If we could suppose the population of Europe to multiply as fast as that of England and Prussia of late years, it would double twice over in a hundred years; that is it would become fourfold what it is now; and this without any deterioration of condition. We English might go on at our present rate of increase, and might draw the additional food from our neighbours, giving our manufactures in return.

But Coal Supply. But at this point arises a very awkward question: Shall we be able to increase our manufactures to four times their present amount? Will the materials be at hand? Above all, will not our coal be exhausted?

XIV.

Professor Jevons's argument, TWO or three years ago, Professor Jevons startled this country, by an elaborate argument, to the effect that our coal supply was being fast exhausted, and that instead of continuing 1,000 or 2,000 years, as we had been accustomed to suppose, it might possibly fail us in a tenth part of that period. The argument, and that of other writers, was summed up by one of the papers as follows:

summed up. Is our supply of coal inexhaustible? and if not, how long will it last? Mr. Jevons enables us to answer both these questions. It is very far from being inexhaustible: it is in process of exhaustion; and, if we go on augmenting our consumption from year to year at our present rate of increase, it will not last a hundred years. Our geological knowledge is now so great and certain, and what we may term the *underground* survey of our islands has been so complete, that we know with tolerable accuracy both the extent, the thickness, and the accessibility of our coal fields, and the quantity of coal annually brought to the surface and used up. The entire amount of coal remaining in Great Britain, down to a depth of 4,000 feet, is estimated to be 80,000 millions of tons. Our annual consumption was in 1860 about 80 millions. At that rate the available coal would last for 1,000 years. But our consumption is now steadily increasing at the rate of $3\frac{1}{2}$ per cent. per annum, and will in 1880 be, not 80 millions, but 160 millions; and, *if it continues thus to increase*, will have worked out the whole 80,000 millions before the year 1960. Nay it would reach this climax probably some time earlier; for our calculation includes all the coal down to 4,000 feet; and no coal mine has yet been worked at a greater depth than 2,500 feet; and we do not believe that mines can be worked profitably, and we have little reason to think they can be worked at all, at such a depth as 4,000 feet.

The writer proceeds to show why in fact the coal will not be thus worked out, because a rise in price will check the consumption: but deferring that question, let us see how far these propositions are true.

Eight propositions.
1. Our coal fields are not inexhaustible.
2. Our geological knowledge is so complete that we know accurately how much coal exists in our island.

3. This quantity is 80,000 millions tons, within 4,000 feet of the surface.

4. In 1860, our consumption was 80 millions tons: therefore we had an underground supply for 1,000 years, supposing no increased rate of consumption.

5. But our rate of consumption has increased and is increasing at $3\frac{1}{2}$ per cent. per annum. It is implied here, that if no new obstacles intervene, this ratio of increase may be expected to continue.

6. If this increasing ratio should continue, the consumption in 1880 will be 160 million tons: and in 1960, if we conceive the same process to go on, all the coal within 4,000 feet will have disappeared.

7. These propositions rest on the hypothesis, that the coal will be got from a depth of 4,000 feet: but at present no coal mine has been sunk deeper than 2,500 feet.

8. Probably no coal mine can be sunk to 4,000 feet, and still more probably it will be unprofitable to go so deep.

Are our coal fields inexhaustible? As to the first proposition, there cannot be two opinions: sooner or later, the coal fields, not only of this island, but of the world, are liable to be worked out. Economists frequently use the same verb in speaking of minerals, and of vegetables or animals: all are said to be produced. No doubt, a man may produce his purse from his pocket: in this sense coal is produced from the mine; it is got out: but wheat is produced by being caused to grow, and we say that wheat is grown. Minerals are got, corn is grown, animals are bred: minerals are *produced*, corn and animals are *reproduced:* the supply of minerals therefore, can be exhausted, the supply of things reproducible is inexhaustible. Every year lessens the quantity of minerals in the ground, every year probably adds, certainly may add, to the quantity of food reproduced. *practically.* This truth is no discovery, and no one will dispute it: the question at issue is quite different. It has hitherto been assumed that the known coal fields of England are so extensive, that with the addition of other English fields probably existing and available, any possible consumption would not exhaust them for a thousand or two thousand years. But to trouble ourselves about the fate of our posterity at so distant a period as two thousand years, would go beyond the most exalted patriotism, and the most ardent desire of *esto perpetua:* we should smile at the notion of a Druid losing a night's rest two thousand years ago, because he foresaw that in the year of grace 1797 great calamities would fall on this island. Prove to men now that our coal will certainly last two thousand years, or even one thousand years, and they will dismiss the subject from their minds; we may apply to distance in time, what Adam Smith in his Moral Sentiments says of distance in space; a man would be more disturbed by having to lose his little finger, than by the certainty that two thousand years hence, all the inhabitants of this island would be without coal or any substitute for it. The interesting question is, whether exhaustion is imminent.

Our geological knowledge. The second statement, that our geological knowledge is complete and that our coal maps are finally made up, is eagerly denied by many. Mr. Holdsworth for example,[*] believes that there are beds of coal where they are not at present even suspected. The *Pall Mall* says of his work[†]:—

---

[*] "Coal under Secondary Formations," 1866.
[†] *Pall Mall Gazette*, Oct. 29, 1866, p. 10.

"If Mr. Holdsworth's theory should prove on extended trial to be as satisfactory as it looks on paper, and as partial trial has shown it to be, the panic respecting a speedy exhaustion of our coal fields may be very considerably allayed. To put it in few words, this writer believes that the fields now in working are but the croppings up of a vast field which underlies the more recent deposits *throughout the whole extent* of the island. This is not a new theory, and Mr. Holdsworth has himself been for some years an exponent of it, but his book comes seasonably at the present time. . . .
There are many reasons for supposing that the coal measures, or alternating beds of coal, slate-clay, and sandstone, may extend uninterruptedly, though perhaps at a great depth, through districts where coal is not found or suspected. Thus the coal fields of Yorkshire resemble so closely those of Northumberland and Durham, that an authority of weight in such matters considers them to be a re-emergence of the same measures, from beneath the covering of magnesian limestone which on the surface divides one field from the other. Under the red marl and new red sandstone of the Midland Counties it is admitted that large tracts of coal measures exist, containing seams of workable coal. Near West Bromwich the ten-yard seam of South Staffordshire lies under Permian rocks. An estate in Durham which is now very valuable from its abundant coal was on the point of being sold at a low price thirty years ago because it was on magnesian limestone, and therefore, it was assumed, could not yield coal. Lord Maynard bored in faith for three years on his Bagworth estates, and at the end of that time his faith was rewarded by the discovery of a rich coal field now in extensive working. Mr. Holdsworth

himself bored for three years—for he is something more than a mere theorist—and finally reached the coal measures, but his boring at that interesting crisis came to an untimely end, in consequence of the fraudulent introduction of steel and iron into the hole."

It cannot then, be justly said that our geological knowledge is complete.

Increased consumption. Of the third and fourth propositions I will say nothing: I will go on to the fifth, which is that our consumption has been increasing at the rate of $3\frac{1}{2}$ per cent. per annum, and has therefore been doubling in about 20 years. According to one account* the rate is even far higher; the annual consumption having risen from $31\frac{1}{2}$ millions in 1845, to 65 in 1858, and as I find elsewhere, to 98 in 1865, and $101\frac{1}{2}$ in 1866; the quantity therefore, having doubled in 13 years and tripled in 20 years. But if it has doubled in 20 years, and if that rate of increase should continue, the annual consumption about 20 years hence will be 200 millions; 40 years hence, 400 millions; 60 years hence, 800 millions; 80 years hence, 1,600 millions: a child now living might thus see our present vast consumption augmented sixteen fold. On this supposition of an unchecked supply, the value of the coal raised would be, at the present prices, about 400 millions £.; or far more than half the present aggregate annual incomes of the nation.

The Times article on it. The *Times*† had a striking article on this particular view of the case: the writer takes the consumption of 1861 as his basis.

"Agreeing to 83 millions of tons as the annual consumption, it is necessary first to divide the total

---

* *Pall Mall Gazette*, April 23, 1866, pa. 7.
† *Times*, May 11, 1866. pa. 6.

quantity into the separate objects of consumption to which it is devoted, and although there are no means for its accurate division, an approximate division will be sufficient.

"The consumption for household purposes is assumed to be a ton for each unit of the population— say 24 millions* of tons a year; and the theory we are considering involves that the consumption of coal for household purposes shall be in 1961, 576 millions of tons, and that, as the country will be neither hotter nor colder, and coals will afford the same warmth to each person, the corresponding population of the British Isles will be also 576 millions.

"The next single item is the consumption of coal for railway travelling, amounting at the present time to about five millions of tons for 10,000 miles of railway within Great Britain. The theory involves that the number of tons supposed to be consumed for this purpose in 1961 will be 120 millions of tons; so that either the railways must extend within Great Britain to 24 times their present length, or the train services must be 24 times their present number, or both compounded must involve the increase of the aggregate consumption.

"The present consumption in the iron trade is about 18 millions of tons of coal, operating to produce and manipulate $4\frac{1}{2}$ millions of tons of pig iron; and the theory involves that the quantity of coal consumed in 1961, for this purpose will be 472 millions of tons, which would produce 24 times the present make of pig iron.

"These three objects employ more than half of the total consumption, and it may be assumed that the

---

* Omitting Ireland I presume, where the quantity used is small, but increasing.

other half is employed in trade purposes, and that an extension of the latter quantity to 24 times its present amount involves an increase of trade, and consequently of wealth, to much more than 24 times its present amount.

"According to the present rate of increase established by the population returns, the total amount of population in 1961 cannot exceed 90 millions, involving a consumption of coal for household purposes of the same number of tons of coal, so that there is a discrepancy between the result of the rate of the increase of consumption of coal of 480 million tons, or five-sixths of the total assumed consumption.

"Few persons will consider that the consumption of coal for railway transit can more than double its present amount, so that there will be a discrepancy under that head of 110 million tons, or more than five-sixths of the assumed consumption. The only one of the three above-mentioned items of which the amount is not limited is the make of iron. This would involve an increase of population employed in that trade from 60,000 to 1,444,000 ; and it may be added that the coal miners must be correspondingly increased in number from 250,000 to 6,000,000 persons. The same proportionate increase must take place in the persons engaged in other trades dependent on the consumption of coal. Taking only three trades—cotton, wool, and silk—at 500,000 persons, their numbers must be increased to 12 millions, irrespective of a corresponding increase in the persons engaged in the trades connected with those manufactures."

Irregularity of increased consumption. I do not pretend to adopt every statement in this article : but I think it cleverly raises the question, whether the alarmists have put the matter fairly. It is certainly true that in the ten years between 1854 and 1864, the consumption has increased by 28 million tons, and this may be an increase at the rate of about $3\frac{1}{2}$ per cent. per annum, which implies a doubling of the consumption in 20 years. But why should the increase be put in this form of a $3\frac{1}{2}$ per cent. reckoned as compound interest is? The object is manifest: it is to obtain a law by which we may read the future: but there is no law unless there is some force operating with regularity; whereas here there is no regularity. The annual increments are as follow:*—

MILLIONS TONS.

Minus 3.	Plus 5.	Minus 1.	0	Plus 7.
1855	1856	1857	1858	1859

Plus 8.	Plus 3.	Minus 2.	Plus 5.	Plus 6.
1860	1861	1862	1863	1864

No *law* of increase can be deduced from such data.

Average increase 3 million tons. It is indisputable that there has been a large increase: amounting on the average of the ten years to about 3 million tons a year. If we take a much longer period, from 1845 to 1864, we find the average increase to be a little larger, being something over 3 millions. Now there is all the difference between a compound $3\frac{1}{2}$ per cent. and a simple annual increase of 3 million tons. A hundred years would multiply our present consumption in the one case to 32-fold, in the other to only 4-fold; since in the one case the consumption would double five times, in the other

---

* Statistical Abstract, xiii., 117.

case our present 100 millions tons (in round numbers) would be augmented by 3 millions in each of the next hundred years.

Arithmetical and geometrical ratios. This distinction between an arithmetical and a geometrical ratio, was made familiar to the world by Malthus. Between 1801 and 1851 the population of England and Wales doubled: other things remaining unchanged, we might expect to see it again doubled by 1901, and again by 1951. But we cannot imagine the home-produced food to multiply endlessly : as it is found physically impossible for an unlimited number of ears of corn to grow together and ripen on a plot of ground. It would require much credulity even to believe, that if we had grown 9 million quarters of wheat in 1801 and 18 millions in 1851, we could make the quantity 27 millions in 1901, and 36 millions in 1951 ; and at the same time produce equally increased quantities of all other agricultural produce. But say we could do this ; we should then have,

	1801.	1851.	1901.	1951.	2001.	
Population	9	18	36	72	144	Millions.
Wheat	9	18	27	36	45	,,

The first of these lines is a geometrical series, the second is an arithmetical series. The alarmists have been pleased to represent the past increase of coal consumption, in the form of the first or geometrical series.

The future : three questions. Let us then content ourselves with the fact that the consumption of coal has increased during 20 years, by about 3 million tons a year. What are our prospects for the future ? May we expect this increase to continue ? We may form a conjectural opinion by inquiring what have been the past causes of the increase ; whether those causes will continue in operation; and whether other causes are likely to counteract them or to cooperate with them.

What has caused the increase? Railroads, I have gone back to 1845: the mention of that year will remind everyone of the immense extension of railroads just then taking place. The success of the Liverpool and Manchester line, opened in 1830, the opening of the Liverpool and Birmingham line, and of part of the London and Birmingham line, both in 1837, had greatly excited the nation: and between 1845 and 1847, we suffered from one of our paroxysms of national insanity. Ever since that period there has been a steady growth of lines in Europe and America, and to a smaller extent in Asia. But Great Britain has supplied a large portion of the rails, engines, and carriages, all of them causing a great consumption of iron and of coal.

Free Trade, and Gold. Immediately afterwards came Sir Robert Peel's conversion to free trade, and the adoption of fiscal measures which have since more than tripled our exports. But these do not consist of wheat, or wool, or timber: they consist of manufactures, all of which require a consumption of coal. Besides this, the gold discoveries made happily about the same time, have marvellously facilitated the multiplied transactions arising out of these changes; and have themselves directly increased our external commerce. The consumption in Great Britain of commodities generally, has been very much augmented: the additional millions of quarters of wheat received annually from Russia and America, have disappeared without any considerable reduction of the average price. The enlarged income of the labouring classes, who have not only earned higher wages, but have also had unusually regular employment, are spent to a great extent on the necessaries of life; and among these, after food fuel is one of the first. Doubtless, if we could ascertain the truth, we should find that far more coal is burnt in small houses now than twenty years ago. In the country too, off the lines of the canals, fuel was formerly cruelly expensive; it is so now in too many parts; but the extension of railroads, which have not generally shut up the canals, has lessened this evil. The *Times*, we have seen, estimated our household consumption at 24 million tons, or a ton a head throughout Great Britain: if in 1845 our whole quantity raised was under 32 millions, it is possible that our household consumption was 16 millions; and it is possible that the 16 may have grown to 24 or to 30. An attempt has been ably made* to calculate the quantities; but it has been found impossible to separate household consumption from that by mills and smiths' forges, though that of the iron trade has been struck out. The London statistics however, may help us. We find that in 1835 London consumed less than $2\frac{1}{2}$ million tons; in 1865, nearly 6 millions: that while the population had far *less* than doubled the consumption had far *more* than doubled. Cheapness has produced its ordinary effect of increased consumption: no doubt this is true of all places distant from the mines; and if true of London, more true of places devoid of supply by water.

During thirty years, our consumption has been stimulated by three mighty changes: the construction of railroads, the adoption of free trade, and the discoveries of gold; three changes, each of which taken separately was enough to produce a financial revolution.

---

* *Birmingham Daily Post*, Nov. 17, 1866.

Will these causes continue? Will these causes continue in operation? I do not mean by this to ask whether we shall return to our old habits: it is impossible that we should surrender railway communication and go back to the turnpike roads;. or that we should revert to protection, while Europe is trying to imitate our new regime: nor is it to be expected that our gold supplies should fail us; since, according to a French authority,* Australia may yield its 13 millions £ annually for the next two thousand years. The question is whether our recent *rate* of progress will continue: whether a further extension of railroads and of foreign commerce, will augment our make of iron in the next ten years by 50 per cent., as happened between 1855 and 1865: whether further cheapness of carriage and further rise of wages and improved regularity of employment, will again multiply our household demand for coal. I see no reason to expect such future increase. As to railroads, the tendency at home, since the commercial crash of 1866, is to lessen to the lowest point all extensions; and therefore to limit the demand for railroad iron to that necessary for replacing what is worn out. As to foreign demand, many persons believe that it will diminish here through increasing supplies furnished abroad. We can scarcely believe that our make of iron will increase during the next ten years as it did during the last ten years.

Not probable. But if our annual consumption of coal should rise during ten years more by 3 million tons a year, and should thus reach 130 millions by 1876, I should still be sceptical as to the indefinite continuance of this augmentation, even if no considerable rise of price takes place. We are

---

* *Revue des deux Mondes*, 66, 400.

told* that 8 years ago, the whole world raised only 121 million tons, of which 72 millions were raised in England, and about half that quantity in the rest of Europe. But there are abundant beds in different parts of Europe, some of which are coming into work.†

"In Germany, we learn from Hamburg that British coal has hitherto been largely imported into Northern Europe; but in Prussia and the interior the case is different, cheapness of the indigenous coal and facilities of transport bid fair to drive English coal out of the market. . . . . The most important supplies are derived from the Westphalian coal fields, the value of which is greatly increased by the proximity to the metal industry. From this quarter we learn that the only limit to production is the deficiency of hands: the production of 1852 having been 38,000,000 of quintals, whilst that of 1864 was 140,000,000; and Westphalian coal is rapidly excluding English from Holland, and is expected to do as much in Northern Germany, by communication viâ the Elbe.

"In Austria, where it is said an unlimited supply of coal might be obtained, the production is only estimated at 4,500,000 tons per annum, half of which is of an inferior quality, but insufficient and expensive means of communication have limited operations. In Russia, also, there are enormous coal fields, of which little profit has as yet been made, from want of skill and of capital. The coal of the Moscow basin is, however, of an inferior quality; but the value of the Oural district is increased by proximity to iron, and that of the Don district by its easy access to the sea of Azoff.

---

* Peto, Resources of America, 187-188; and Annals Brit. Legisl. Oct. 1866, 439. † *Economist*, February 10, 1866.

"It is needless however, to remark that the coal fields to which we have referred are as nothing compared with those of North America. In Pennsylvania—the largest producer both of anthracite and bituminous coal—the value of coal mined has increased in ten years at the rate of 179 per cent., whilst the corresponding increase in *all* the States is estimated at 186 per cent."

It may be a moderate consolation to an Englishman to learn that the world at large has coal enough for thousands of years, if at the same time it appears that that of his own country threatens exhaustion in a hundred years: but the existence of these extensive beds in other countries, the fast spreading means of carriage by railway, and the rapid growth of international communication, which is conducting English and French capital into every corner of Europe, lead to the conclusion that continental coal, and perhaps continental iron, will soon enter into a brisk competition with those of Great Britain, and will thus reduce the further increase of our consumption. Landlords and miners and ironmasters, may regret such a check to their royalties and profits and wages: but the rest of the country may rejoice in the diminished danger of rapid exhaustion.

Supply may be increased: limit 4,000 feet. Again; not only may the consumption turn out far less than has been anticipated, but the supply may turn out much greater. I have shown that there are great differences of opinion as to the geological formations in which coal is likely to be found. There are also differences of opinion as to the depth to which we can descend. The alarmists say we cannot go below 4,000 feet: this limit is disputed. It is true* that the lowest depth we English have

---

* *Economist*, January 6, 1866, pa. 5.

reached, is 2,500 feet (nearly half a mile) but at Kitzbühl,* in the Tyrol, there is a mine 2,763 feet; and† at Gilly, near Charleroy, there is one of 3,411 feet.

Increased heat. It has been supposed that below 4,000 feet the heat would become intolerable. Mr. Vivian, in his remarkable speech to the House of Commons, confesses that the temperature rises as we descend into the earth, but he ridicules the notion of our not being able to overcome the difficulty‡ by mechanical means. The subject is discussed also by Mr. Warrington Smyth;§ who says that below 10 or 20 yards from the surface, the temperature increases at the rate of 1° Fahr. for every 60 or 70 feet of descent: that the first opening of drifts even at 1,500 to 2,000 feet is a hot task; but that the temperature sinks rapidly by the circulation of external air. The *Revue des deux Mondes*‖ makes the rate of increase one degree centigrade for 30 metres; which is not very far from Mr. Smyth's statement.

Cost. But an uninitiated person would naturally suppose, that the expense of sinking a very deep pit would be an insuperable obstacle. Mr. Vivian contends that this is an utter mistake. He says that though the first cost of sinking is great, it is only a trifle per ton on the coal got: he says that a single mine may yield 60 million tons of coal, and that therefore one penny a ton would recoup so unheard of an outlay as 250,000 £. The additional cost of drawing to the surface is very small: far less than a penny a ton. But even if we triple that, three

---

* *Pall Mall Gazette*, October 29, 1866, pa. 10.
† Warrington W. Smyth, "Coal and Coal Mining," 246.
‡ Speech of H. Hussey Vivian, Esq., M.P., June 12, 1866, Ridgway, p. 13.
§ "Coal and Coal Mining," 245.   ‖ No. 72, pa. 1,004.

pence a ton is a matter of small importance. At the beginning of this century, best coal was, as I hear,* sold in Birmingham at 8s.; the present price is more than 12s.: a rise of 4s. a ton has not checked the manufacturers' prosperity: a certainty of an additional three pence would fail even to cause uneasiness.

Importance of the limit. But the existence of such a limit as 4,000 feet makes all the difference in the question. Mr. Vivian says† :—"That limit of 4,000 feet, cuts off at one fell swoop from the coal field of South Wales, the gigantic quantity of 24 thousand millions of tons. That is the quantity of coal which Mr. Hull calculates to be below this imaginary and arbitrary limit of 4,000 feet, beyond which it is represented that operations cannot be pushed. These 24,000 millions of tons would actually supply the present enormous consumption of England for nearly 300 years." This is said of South Wales taken singly, but the same is true of other coal fields; and therefore, if we can get coal to indefinite depths, the fears of exhaustion cease.

Conclusion of the 8 propositions. I have now gone through the eight propositions which I found in the summary I quoted. I conclude (1) that though our coal fields are exhaustible, it is impossible for us to determine whether they will be exhausted in any such period as to affect the well-being of the nation: (2) that our knowledge of the coal existing underground is far from complete: (3) that our consumption has undoubtedly increased very fast; having grown by one half in 10 or 11 years, and having perhaps grown threefold in 20 years: (4) that

---

* In 1769, after the Canal to the collieries was opened, the price was 6s. to 7s. per ton of 2,240 lbs. Langford's "Century," 178-179.
† Speech 7.

this growth has been irregular, not implying any law which may enable us to predict the future ; that it has taken place during three great changes; during the formation of railroads, during the adoption of free trade with a consequent vast extension of production, and during the discoveries of Californian and Australian gold; that we have no reason to anticipate further changes of the same kind, and that though the adoption of free trade by other nations may tend to still further multiply our exports, there is a probability of a check to our exportation both of coal and of iron, by the opening of mines in several European countries : (5) that the limit of 4,000 feet as the alleged greatest depth from which coal can be won, is arbitrary and not founded on experience; and that it cannot be sustained on the ground of increasing heat, or the augmented cost of sinking shafts and raising the coal.

Substitutes. It is really believed, no doubt, that if coal should fail something else will take its place. The subjoined reply * is, I think, conclusive :—

" Some persons solace themselves with a vague fancy that science will discover some substitute for coal, some new motive power, some new source of light and heat. It *may* do so ; but it is of no use to discuss dreams, or to build our future hopes for the rescue of Great Britain from impending fall, on so unfounded a ' perhaps.' We need only make two remarks on this suggestion : first, it is not impossible, nor indeed improbable, that *light* may be obtained in some hitherto undreamed of mode—perhaps even heat for our dwellings ;—but who anticipates a new fuel which shall be abundant and cheap enough to supply our smelting furnaces ? and, secondly, what

---

* *Pall Mall Gazette*, April 21, 1866, pa. 5.

probability is there that any substitute for coal whether in the generation of steam or the feeding of furnaces, will be discovered in these islands *specially*, or in any form that will give us our present advantage over other countries ?"

French scientific men have been speculating on this interesting topic : the following passage* has unintentionally a touch of Swift.

" What can be done afterwards ? Wood and petroleum offer very insufficient resources. Must we think of decomposing the rocks which contain carbonates in order to extract from them the combustible matter *par excellence ?* M. Simonin suggests an original solution : he says *we must bottle up the sun*. Solar radiation has formed plants, and consequently fossil coal ; let us seek directly the heat which it affords us in such large quantities. What is to prevent us for example, from heating balls of clay by means of reflecting mirrors, and from thus storing up heat, as cold is stored up in ice houses ? We concede to M. Simonin that the heat sent us by the sun is immense, for it appears from the experiments of M. Pouillet, that the earth receives from it annually *un septillion de calories ;* of which the atmosphere absorbs about half, and the remainder penetrates the soil, and is equal to the heat produced by the combustion of 60 to 80 trillions of tons of coal: this is three or four hundred thousand times as much as is got from coal mines ; but how are we to fix this heat, which is disseminated over a surface of a hundred thousand millions of acres ? A different solution, we think, is required. Instead of continuing to seek our mechanical force from the heat of furnaces which supply our machines, we shall

---

* *Revue des deux Mondes*, 1st January, 1867, p. 252.

end by seeking it from some other natural force. Electricity indeed, gives little promise of superseding steam; but there are many other forces which man has not yet *tamed*: to mention only one, the tides of the ocean await their Watt and their Fulton."

I cannot see that a Watt or a Fulton is wanted to tame the forces of the ocean. A tidal river appears to furnish the means of filling at the flow, a lake which would turn mill wheels at the ebb. Unfortunately the power is in the wrong place: it is confined to the coast, and cannot be conveyed to the mines and to the other centres of industry.

XV.

Some ground for fear. ON the whole, I believe that the fears of a failure of coal have been exaggerated; but I cannot deny that there is considerable uncertainty: we are constantly exhausting our principal, and we cannot replace it; nor can we determine absolutely how soon penury may overtake us.

We should still be great in agriculture: Even if our manufacturing superiority should come to an end, we should probably remain a very great nation. We were great in the time of Louis XIV., and in the Spanish war, and in the Seven Years' War, when we were an agricultural people: we should still be great if we became an agricultural people again. Probably if our manufactures and commerce declined, our unemployed capital would flow over the land, and improve our farming to the utmost, just as happened in Holland after the decline of its commercial predominance.

"She,* who had beaten Spain, and had gloriously resisted the combined forces of France and England, sank gradually as we know, under the fatal attacks of a war of tariffs. Differential duties and the Navigation Act drove her shipping out of every port; her commerce was annihilated, her marine destroyed. At the end of the eighteenth century, Holland had fallen into most distressing weakness, and the French conquest, under the empire, consummated her ruin by transferring her colonies to England. Just at that moment however, agriculture, hitherto despised, opened to her new sources of wealth. It has often happened that politicians, ministers, or even monarchs, fallen from power, have renewed their youth in rural pursuits, and have found consolation in the thought of contributing in a modest fashion to fertilise their native soil and to promote the welfare of their fellows. As with men so with nations. Has their lot been unprosperous, have they sunk in an unequal contest, have their commerce and industry waned under the influence of opposing events, there still remains to them an inexhaustible source of gain and well being which will retrieve all their losses, which will heal their wounds, and which will not be dried up by the fortune of war or the vicissitudes of treaties: this source is the soil, fairly made use of and always ready to recompense tenfold whatever intelligent sacrifices men can resolve to make; in a word it is agriculture. This it is in fact which formerly supported Lombardy and Belgium, while subject to a foreign power and robbed of their old pursuits; and this it is also which more recently has raised Holland when fallen from her ancient commercial greatness."

---

* Émile de Laveleye, La Néerlande, 1865, pa. 254.

and from our national character. I do not dispute that our national resources during the last hundred years have been greatly increased by manufactures and commerce: I believe however, that below these there is something which has made the nation great; which made it great for centuries before its manufactures were considerable, and when the Genoese and the Dutch crowed over us at sea. Industry, integrity, and long-continued freedom ; a soil rugged but strong, a climate unpleasing but temperate ; an insular position defended by stubborn courage: these are qualities and gifts independent of mining and manufactures and commerce, and these secure our greatness though coal and iron should fail us.

Greatness and prosperity not the same. But greatness and prosperity are not the same thing. The Dutch have for three centuries had a national greatness: their dogged resolution, their industry, their frugality, have enabled them to bear up against adversity, and to recover from overwhelming misfortune. But they have have had to endure adversity and overwhelming misfortune: the loss of their commerce, the unmerited hostility of Louis XIV., the irresistible conquest by Napoleon. We too, though we may continue great, must expect misfortune : what it may be, who shall say ?

War. At the present moment, no dark cloud hangs over us. But it is impossible to say how soon we may be drawn into the vortex of European war; and that unbroken peace is likely to prevail in Europe, it is hard to believe: Russia indeed, is busy with her emancipated peasants; and both she and Austria are cowed by the defeats of the last few years: France and Prussia however, have an unsettled account to liquidate; for French patriots bear unwillingly the glory of other nations.

XVI.

CONCLUSIONS.

IN this second part, I have inquired whether there are in this country, any circumstances which modify the general rules as to debt. I admit that the money borrowed, having been spent, cannot be recovered: that the credit of our government is so good as to require no propping up: that the burden of our taxation though heavy is not intolerable: that there may be cases in which a sinking-fund would be a mistake; as for example in the United States, where the first thing to be done is to regulate the taxation, so levied at present as to press on the springs of industry. But I contend that nevertheless, a sinking-fund is needed in Great Britain: because our escape from that national insolvency which has humiliated most other countries, is not owing to our honesty alone, but very much to the good fortune that has attended us; to Watt and Arkwright, and the extension of our manufactures, followed by a marvellous increase of population and opulence. I maintain that it is preposterous to anticipate the perpetual recurrence of such favourable circumstances; and while I rejoice that during the last thirty years the debt has grown but little, I hold that this is not enough. I do not pretend to look with alarm on the *immediate* future: I believe that in the extension of free trade among other nations, and in the development by railways of the agricultural resources of Eastern Europe, there are hopes for Great Britain of a still further extension of manufactures and commerce, though chequered by our augmenting dependence on foreigners for our bread:

I do not even share the alarm expressed as to the probable failure of our coal during the next century; since I cannot see the probability of a return of such causes of increase as our adoption of free trade and our construction of railways, and our discoveries of gold, all of which have operated principally during the last twenty years. On the other hand, the more distant future is less bright. Manufacturing predominance is in its very nature transitory: our supply of coal must some time or other fail, and the cost of mining increases a little every year: we have had a long period of singular prosperity, but to rely on its continuance for centuries to come would be madness. The fertility of our soil, the happiness of our climate, the strength of our character, the freedom and flexibility of our political institutions, the increased tenderness of our affluent classes towards the poor and distressed, our growing distaste for war and glory, our willingness to surrender our colonies so soon as they prove fit to go alone, all give us reason to hope for continued national greatness. But national greatness and national prosperity are not the same thing. Without any falling-off of our population and opulence, we may lose our national predominance. In a stationary or slowly increasing condition we may experience, as Holland has experienced, a sense of national stagnation. Surely, before those evil days come upon us, we ought to make arrangements for removing a burden which may then be scarcely endurable.

211

XVII.

PART III.

Would a sinking-fund correct the evils of debt?

The evil of paying over and over again.

WE have seen that the first and greatest of the many evils attending a national debt, is the having to pay it over and over again in the form of interest.

If I am fortunate enough to come into possession of an estate of 2,000 £ a year, and I determine to lay out 10,000 £ on a house and furniture, I may do this by applying to it the 2,000 £ a year for 5 years; living in the meantime on the income from other sources which had sufficed me before: in this case I incur no debt. But I may do it also, by borrowing the 10,000 £ at 5 per cent.; in this case I shall have to pay 500 £ a year. My income is permanently reduced to 1,500 £. At the end of 20 years, if I have discharged none of the principal, I shall have paid for interest 20 times 500 £, or 10,000 £; the sum I borrowed: at the end of 40 years, I and my heir, will have paid 20,000 £; twice the sum I borrowed; and at the end of 100 years, the family, if they hold the estate on the same terms, will have paid 5 times the sum I borrowed. Dr. Price would represent the loss as something vastly greater than this; because we might have invested these sums at compound interest, and thus calculated, what we had paid for interest would amount to hundreds of thousands of pounds. Now, however improbable it may seem that such an estate, charged with such a sum, should remain unchanged in one family during a hundred years, there is no improbability that a nation should continue with the same debts during much longer periods than a hundred years : in truth the sums borrowed under William III. are still owing ; and the interest on each million has amounted to six or eight millions, besides our being still under an obligation to pay an annuity until the million is discharged.

XVIII.

What might be done? A YOUNG and vivacious people like the Americans, if they were circumstanced as we are, being once convinced of this simple truth, would resolve to make a great effort.
The sacrifice necessary. If it were asked what sacrifice would be necessary to extinguish the debt, it would be replied that in a country where 5 per cent. was the current rate of interest, a sinking-fund of 10 millions £ a year, with compound interest, would amount to our 800 millions £ in 33 years. In Great Britain, where interest is lower, a longer period would be necessary.
Could we raise 10 millions £ a year? We see that 10 millions £ a year, would extinguish our debt in a period not very long in the life of a nation. Could we raise such a sum? If we deemed the proposed object a really important one, no doubt we could. In the early part of the century, when we felt that Napoleon must be put down, we consented to an income tax of 2s. in the £, in addition to heavy imposts on nearly every article, down to salt itself. How the pressure of that 2s. in the £ was felt, is shown by the hurried way in which it was cast off on the return of peace. Of late years, on a much lighter

occasion, when our existence and our liberties were in no wise threatened; I mean during the Crimean war, when the honour of our armies, once engaged, was the only subject of anxiety to the ordinary public, we paid without complaint 1s. 4d. in the £. Three-fourths of that rate, half of the rate paid by our fathers, would furnish the needed 10 millions £ a year. This added to what we already pay, would make 1s. in the £. If we could resolve to bear such a burden, we should make an effort worthy of a young, fresh, enterprising, and patriotic people; and we should actually follow the admirable example of Holland, though still at a humble distance; and we should see a hope of arriving some time or other, by the straight road too, at the happy condition of Prussia and Sweden in freedom from debt.

Utopian. I am not utopian enough to recommend, or to hope for, any scheme so spirited, so thorough, so patriotic. People will not be persuaded that the object is worth the sacrifice. They simply will not pay the money; and they will clothe their resolution in some form such as this.

First objection: increase of population and wealth: Population and wealth, it will be said, are steadily rising: in England and Wales, the richest part of the kingdom, population doubled in the fifty years between 1801 and 1861; and though the *rate* of increase is less than it has been, the absolute numbers added in each year, are at least as great as those of any former period: the means of paying taxes also, have certainly grown at a greater rate than the population. If, after the peace of Amiens, our fathers had made a great effort to pay off the large debt contracted, they would have made, for every million they raised, a sacrifice three or four times as great as that now imposed on us to raise that million: in the same way, if we made the considerable sacrifice necessary to raise 10 millions £ a year, our grandsons might say that if we had left it to them, they could have raised the money with a third or a fourth of the difficulty.

assumes that the future will be like the past. This argument assumes that the future circumstances of England will exactly resemble the present, and those which are lately past. Population and wealth indeed, will probably go on increasing: but who knows what draughts there may be upon the means of our posterity? what wars, what pestilences, what series of bad harvests, what growth of foreign competition in manufactures? A man who prophesies all or any of these, is a fanatic: a man who denies the possibility, or even the probability, of some of them, is a fool. I have no fear for the greatness of our country, because I see that it is founded on the happiness of her geographical position, on the power of her institutions to adapt themselves to changing circumstances, and above all, on the moral strength of the people, a strength developed by centuries of good and free government. But greatness and prosperity, as I have said before, are not necessarily conjoined: England was never greater than in 1797, when the successes of the French Revolution, the mutiny of the Nore, and the suspension of the Bank of England, made the boldest men tremble. This greatness we may have to display again. And in such future periods, instead of regretting that the subjects of Queen Victoria made sacrifices to lessen the debt, the subjects of a King Albert, or of a George V., will curse the careless selfishness of their progenitors, who preferred ease to patriotism.

I therefore repudiate the opinion that we may leave sinking-funds to our posterity, because they may perhaps be better able to establish them.

Growth indicates prosperity. Again; why is it that population and opulence are growing? It is because the nation is in the enjoyment of prosperity. To say then, that a sinking-fund shall be deferred until growth has ceased, is to say that it shall be deferred till a time of adversity. A mine-owner with an increasing income from royalties, will not begin to pay his debts, because in ten years' time his enlarged income will make the payment much easier: when the ten years have passed, his mines are less productive and his income falls off: he is then conscious of his folly which could not anticipate so obvious a probability. If we mean to pay off our debt, let us begin to-day, while our prosperity is indicated by an increase of population and opulence.

If adversity should come. At present we are importing a large part of the food we consume: we pay for it with manufactures. Suppose that foreign competition should narrow our markets, and considerably reduce the prices of goods. Our mechanics might prefer emigration to poverty: an English exodus such as the recent Irish one is possible though improbable: more than a fourth of the Irish have disappeared from their country; what if six millions of English and Scotch passed over to Canada and Australia? Would that be a time for establishing a sinking-fund? The present period, the period of growth, is the only time for reducing our debt.

Second objection; gold discoveries. Other objectors will say, that in the present uncertain state of the standard of value, it would be injudicious to make any considerable effort: they believe that Australia and California and Nevada, are so deluging the world with gold and silver, that a serious depreciation in the value of those precious metals must follow: that our children and grandchildren will therefore have to pay the interest of the debt, and such part of the principal as they may choose to discharge, in a currency of less value than the present; and that it would be improvident on our part to settle with the national creditors now that gold and silver are at a comparatively high value.

Not apply to a gradual payment. A whole chapter would be scarcely sufficient for the discussion of the points raised by this argument. If I were maintaining the propriety of our making a great effort to pay off the whole principal in a few years : if I were recommending the scheme of raising 10 millions £ a year by an additional eightpenny income tax; which as I have shown, might extinguish the debt in a long generation : I should feel the objection to be at least a specious one, and such as unanswered would be fatal. As however, I have no expectation of seeing any such present sacrifice made, and as all that I recommend is the establishment of a fund to discharge the present debt in several generations, it is unnecessary to reply to the objections at any length.

Anticipations falsified. It will be enough to point out that the anticipations of economists have been singularly falsified. The late Mr. Tooke, perhaps the soundest thinker of his day on such subjects, looked with alarm at the few annual millions of Siberian gold,* and feared that they would disturb the standard of European value. Siberia still sends her few millions; and in addition, we have six or seven times as much from the new mines. After this has gone on during a dozen years, it is disputed whether the standard of value has been

---

* I make this assertion from memory, as I cannot find my reference to the passage in Tooke.

disturbed; and whether the rise of prices in various articles has not resulted from the increase of demand, consequent on the extension of commerce by free trade and railroads; facilitated no doubt, by the gold and silver, which appeared just in time to furnish the additional currency wanted for the multiplied transactions.

England: wheat not risen. It should be remembered also, that whatever changes may have taken place throughout the world, the average price of wheat in England has not risen; the free trade in corn having perhaps, counteracted the tendency to rise caused by the abundance of the precious metals. The mainstay of the labourer remains unchanged in price; and where wages have risen, they have not been forced up by that rise in the price of food which naturally follows from a depreciated currency. As regards bread, and the standard of wages, and those prices which are influenced by the standard of wages, we are as though no depreciation of the currency has taken place; whether it has taken place or not.

No considerable effect having followed at present, so far as Great Britain is concerned, it would be foolish to postpone an important arrangement for paying our debts, because we fear that the few millions we should raise would cost a rather less sacrifice to our sons or our grandsons.

Third objection: reform of taxation more important. The third objection I have mentioned before. The evils of a national debt are frankly conceded: it is acknowledged too, that it is highly desirable to establish a sinking-fund. But it is contended that there is another object of still higher importance: the better distribution of taxation; the carrying out of the fiscal reforms begun by Sir Robert Peel, and continued by Mr. Gladstone. We are reminded that twenty-five years ago the elasticity of the revenue had ceased : that it was not then an easy thing for the Chancellor of the Exchequer to raise a sufficient revenue to meet the modest expenditure of the Government. Since then, what a change ! One tax after another has been reduced or repealed, and yet there is always a surplus ; though the peace establishment of army and navy would have been formerly thought large enough for a state of moderate war. Let us proceed in this wise course, which has led to unexampled prosperity, and let us defer the establishment of a sinking-fund till we have banished every tax which weighs upon the springs of industry.

Exaggeration pointed out. I am not at all disposed to underrate the importance of recent fiscal legislation: I value most highly the measures which have given liberty of production and exchange. But it seems to me a mistake to regard those measures as principally a remission of taxation. The laws which limited the importation of corn and cattle, were not framed for the purpose of raising a revenue for government, but for the purpose of protecting the landlords against a fall of rents. When foreign bread and meat were put within the reach of the labouring classes, the thing done was very different from the subsequent measures which reduced tea 1s. a lb., and kid gloves 1s. a pair : the thing done was the putting in the power of our mechanics and capitalists, to exchange their cloth and hardware, for the wheat of the Far West and the oxen of Holstein. If any further removal of such obstacles remains to be accomplished, by all means let us accomplish that even in preference to establishing a sinking-fund : but let us not confound the removal of obstacles and the remission of taxation: let us not suppose that the reduction of the price of tea by 3d. a lb. or of beer by 1d. a quart, will give that kind of elasticity to our resources, which followed from the facilities offered by free trade for international exchange of productions.

But even if no exaggeration: Income-tax. But even if I am wrong in charging these objectors with exaggeration, if it be true that certain remaining taxes are considerable obstacles to production and international exchange, I still contend that a sinking-fund may be established with advantage, and without preventing the repeal of any of those objectionable taxes. There is one tax which interferes neither with production nor with international exchange: I mean the Income Tax. Let us resort to this for our fund.

XIX.

CONCLUSIONS.

I HAVE not feared to incur the risk of tediousness, by pointing out once more, in this Third Part, that the greatest evil of debt is the having to pay it over and over again in the form of interest. I have then shown that if, following the example of Holland, we raised a surplus taxation of 10 millions £ a year, and if this sum were placed out at compound interest, we should soon extinguish our debt. Not that I venture to propose any such scheme : I know that the following objections would be raised : —

1. That by the steady increase of population and opulence, the debt is virtually diminishing; and that it is better to leave its extinction to the enlarged means of future generations : to which I reply that it is folly to expect the continuance of the last

century's good fortune; and that to leave the extinction till growth has ceased, is to decline in prosperous times, a duty to which stagnant and unprosperous times will prove unequal.

2. That the discoveries of gold and silver will raise prices generally, and will in the same proportion lessen the weight of the debt, which may therefore be paid off hereafter at a less sacrifice to the public. I answer that all the predictions as to the effects of the discoveries of the precious metals, have hitherto been falsified: that if the prices of the world have risen, a counteraction has taken place in England, where wheat, the mainstay of life, has been kept down to its old level, through the novel freedom of importation: that even if the anticipated growth of prices should take place, it would be formidable only in case of a proposal to discharge the debt at once, or very early; but that it is of little importance as opposed to a scheme for discharging the debt gradually in the course of a hundred years.

3. That granting the desirability of extinguishing the debt, another change is far more desirable: the further reform of taxation. I reply that the two changes are not incompatible; for that all I propose is to raise a moderate sum by instalments during a few years, and that this could be done by a small addition to the income-tax, without the least interference with reform of taxation.

CHAPTER VI.

HOW WE SHALL BEST PERFORM OUR DUTY.

I.

What ruined Mr. Pitt's scheme? HAVING determined in the last chapter that we are really bound to take measures for repayment of our debt, let us consider what would be the best means of performing that duty: and to do this let us once more recollect what it was that frustrated Mr. Pitt's efforts of 1786.

The S.-F. was not understood by the nation. The first and greatest evil, I suspect, was that the scheme was not understood by the nation. No doubt, the aim of the scheme was plain enough. After the conclusion of peace in 1783, the nation was painfully impressed with the magnitude of the debt, and with the necessity of reduction: it was willing to submit to some additional taxation for this purpose: both parties in parliament agreed in the necessity of action: Mr. Pitt, on introducing his measure, declared it useless to prove the advisability of establishing a sinking-fund, because everyone conceded it. All this was intelligible; as was also the proposition to raise taxes of a million a year to constitute the fund. *Why?* The ambiguity arose in the mode of applying the million. If it had been used to pay off some of the fund-holders, the debt would have been obviously diminished. It would have been equally obvious that in the next year the nation would escape the payment of interest on the discharged million; and could therefore afford in the second year to pay off 1,050,000 £., assuming 5 per cent. to be the government rate of interest at the time. The course pursued was less simple: the million was handed to Commissioners; who bought stock, and had it transferred to their names in trust for the nation. In the second year the £50,000 interest on the million was paid by government to the Commissioners, who again received a million from the taxes, and again bought stock with this million, as well as with the 50,000 £., paid to them for interest.

Even this was intelligible: the nation owed 250 million £., but it possessed in the hands of the Commissioners what was saleable in the market for more than 2 million £. As it was expressed, the debt was 250 millions £., of which more than 2 millions £. was redeemed.

War loans. If peace had continued, the nation might have gone on, clearly understanding that though the debt continued unchanged in amount, a new portion was redeemed each year: but the breaking-out of war introduced a hopeless complication. Suppose that war had broken out in the second year, and that government had become a borrower. Under the clause introduced in 1786, by Mr. Fox, the Commissioners, instead of buying stock, might lend their money directly to government, by which means they would become possessed of newly created stock for the amount lent. The whole process thus became puzzling: a million was raised by taxation, was handed to the Commissioners, who handed it back to the government, together with 50,000 £., also received from government as interest.

Why sinking-fund not suspended. We have already seen the reason for this arrangement: it was thought that the National Debt would be understood to be greater by this million or more, and that in the annual budget the interest for this enlarged debt would be provided : whereas if the million thus bandied about had simply been applied to the current expenditure, it would have disappeared. It is probable that if the war had lasted only one year, and that at once the ordinary course of prosperity had returned, the arrangement would have answered the end proposed. But whether it would so or not, the nation could not follow the steps of the process, and the sinking-fund ceased to be under the guardianship of public opinion.

It seems to me therefore, that the attempt to add to the sinking-fund during a time of loans, was a mistake : that whenever government had to borrow it would have been wiser to take for current expenditure, the million raised by taxation in peace time for the sinking-fund. The nation would then have understood that during war time the sinking-fund was suspended.

II.

New plan must be intelligible, IN considering therefore, what would be the best scheme for the future, I should require in the first place that it should be simple enough for everyone to understand it, and that it should thus be placed under the guarantee of public opinion; the only guarantee which will permanently and steadily maintain its efficiency.

and therefore not one of terminable annuities. For this reason I object to all propositions for converting Consols into terminable annuities; propositions which are also decried, as I have already shown, on the ground of the heavy loss that would be caused, by substituting an inconvenient and unpopular stock for a well established and highly marketable one. One of these schemes was proposed in 1866 at Manchester by Mr. Frederic Hill, from whom I differ unwillingly, because of my entire agreement with him in the main purpose of his paper. I give the text of Mr. Hill's plan.*

Example of a recent scheme of terminable annuities.

"Under the following arrangements the whole debt might be paid off in 124 years:—

"I would propose that next year 100 millions of the permanent three per cent. annuities be converted into five per cent. terminable annuities; to do which would require, for a period of thirty-one years, an addition of about £2,080,000 to the taxes, viz., two millions for interest, and about £80,000 for cost of collection; but from this sum would have to be deducted first nearly £600,000 for existing terminable annuities, which will come to an end next April, and upwards of £700,000, which in like manner, will have to be struck off in nineteen years. Thus the immediate increase in taxation, or rather, let us hope, at least as regards part, the immediate non-reduction of taxation, would be about a million and a half, while in 1885 this sum would be reduced to less than £800,000.

"In 1898 the account would stand as follows: Debt, included estimated equivalent of probable amount of life annuities, about 710 millions, bearing an interest of somewhat more than 21 millions, or, including the cost of collection and management, of about 22 millions; as compared with the present payment of 27 millions, or the payment after 1885 of about 25⅔ millions.

---

* Social Science Transactions, 1866. 685.

"Considering that the country will, in all probability, be much richer in thirty-two years than it is now, and considering that, from an advance in education and public morality, the impulse which now urges us to pay off the National Debt will no doubt be stronger, I trust that when the year 1898 arrives there will be a general willingness to employ at least the greater part of this saving, say three millions, in a further conversion of permanent into terminable annuities. If this be done, under the same arrangement as the first proposed conversion, it would apply to a sum of 150 millions; and in thirty-one more years the debt would be brought down to about 560 millions; requiring a taxation of about $17\frac{1}{2}$ millions, or about $4\frac{1}{2}$ millions less than in 1898, and nearly $9\frac{1}{2}$ millions less than now."

By continuing this process, as Mr. Hill shows, the whole debt would be extinguished in less than 130 years.

Objection. I do not stop to inquire how far this scheme would be interfered with by the inevitable wars and loans of the next 130 years; nor what would be the exact amount of the heavy loss attending the conversion of 800 millions £. of perpetual annuities into terminable annuities; nor what would be the inconvenience to the money market of having for investment, not perpetual annuities but terminable annuities, the value of which would diminish daily; nor the trouble to trustees and to the Court of Chancery, who would have to divide every annual sum they received into interest and principal, the interest to be paid to the beneficiary and the principle to be reinvested.

Waiving all these difficulties, I rest upon one paramount objection; that this and other similar schemes are complex, and to the many unintelligible: that therefore, any Chancellor of the Exchequer, in preparing his annual budget, might trench on the provisions made without awakening any alarm outside the House: that in short, the scheme would not be under the guarantee of public opinion: the only guarantee I could trust.

III.

Actual plan: not direct extinction. WHAT scheme would be intelligible? The obvious one is to apply the sinking-fund each year to paying off debt. A million is raised: if Consols were at par, the million £ would pay off a million of Consols; if Consols were at 80, the million £ would pay off $1\frac{1}{4}$ millions of Consols. So much debt would be extinguished. The next year, as the nation would escape the interest on the million extinguished, the sum applicable to the sinking-fund would be increased by £30,000 or more. This process carried on, would bring into play the principle of compound interest.

But even this arrangement would scarcely possess the desired simplicity; and I fear that a Chancellor, proposing to repeal an obnoxious tax, would obtain the consent of the nation to abandon the annual increase in the sinking-fund, and to confine it to a fixed amount; that is to give up the principle of compound interest. If this principle is to be strictly observed, the provision for the sinking-fund should ultimately not appear at all in the budget: it should be out of the competency of the Chancellor of the Exchequer to meddle with the fund.

Public understands govern- The public perfectly understands that the government may possess property:

ment possession of property. that it does in fact possess ships which are saleable, old stores, woods, rights of treasure trove, sums lent to landlords and secured on their estates; that the Belgian government possesses the rights of royalties in mines, and a valuable property in railroads. The public would perfectly understand an account stating that the government, on behalf of the nation, owed 800 millions £, but possessed property worth 15 millions £; and that during the past year the property had increased from 12 to 15 millions £. This was not so clear when it was said that the debt was 800 million £, of which the sum of 200 million £ was redeemed: it would have been perfectly clear if the 200 million £ had been invested in lands and canals and mortgages.

If then, with equal money profit, the Commissioners of the National Debt could invest in securities outside government stocks, I should regard that change as highly favourable to the permanence of a sinking-fund, as exempting it from the danger of being tampered with by a perplexed Chancellor of the Exchequer. I would have the fund established once for all, and free from the dangers of an annual parliamentary vote.

Should not however, buy property. I would not however, recommend that the Commissioners should go into the market and buy freehold properties or railroads or mineral rights: such purchases would probably be made badly, and would certainly be open to censorious criticism. Fixed money securities would suit our purpose much better. The Commissioners would do just what the great Insurance Companies do: what the Globe has done in the case of a million £ put in trust for the payment of 6 per cent. annuities; what the Scottish Widows' Fund has done with its large accumulations amounting to more than 4 millions £.

The Commissioners would have to lend for long fixed periods : they could lend for drainage and other improvements on Irish lands held under the safe titles granted by the Landed Estates' Court: they would be free from the necessity of requiring rapid repayment.

What rate of interest could be obtained? If there should be a pecuniary loss by this mode of investment, that would be fatal to my proposal, just as it is fatal to the scheme of turning Consols into terminable annuities. But I conjecture that there would be no loss, and that there would be even a considerable gain. For I find that large sums are so invested as to yield a higher rate than that paid by the government on Consols, which we may call $3\frac{1}{4}$ per cent. (taking the price of Consols at 92). Now we all know that in private trusts, without any violation of the legal provisions, an average interest of $4\frac{1}{2}$ or even $4\frac{3}{4}$ per cent. is obtained, by lending in moderate amounts, and buying freehold ground rents, and taking the best railway debentures. I concede that the largeness of the sums with which the Commissioners would have to deal, would rather lower this rate. The insurance companies however, whose amounts are considerable, gain interest far above the $3\frac{1}{4}$ per cent. of Consols. The Scottish Widows' Fund have property amounting to 4 or 5 millions £.* Before 1860† the average rate of interest realized was about 4 per cent. Since that time it has been :—

	£	s.	d.	
In 1860	4	1	3	per £100
„ 1861	4	2	5	„
„ 1862	4	3	0	„
„ 1863	4	2	10	„
„ 1864	4	4	3	„
„ 1865	4	7	0	„
„ 1866	4	10	6	„

---

* 53rd Annual Report, 23. col. 1.   † *Ib.* 10.

It may seem that there is no reason why the Commissioners of the sinking-fund should not earn a rate approaching that of such a company: and that therefore, instead of having a loss of interest by the adoption of my scheme, we might rather hope to make a considerable profit by it.

An Actuary's opinion. A distinguished Actuary has given me the following information :—

"Insurance Companies hold, at the lower end of the scale, investments in government funds at about $3\frac{1}{4}$ per cent.; deposits at Joint Stock Banks, now producing 1 per cent. only, but averaging perhaps 3 per cent., *communibus annis;* deposits at private banks, and moneys in agents' hands, as unproductive balances. Then at the other and higher end of the scale, investments on mortgage at about $4\frac{1}{2}$ per cent.; on life interests with insurance at 5 per cent.; advances to municipalities, local boards &c., $4\frac{1}{2}$ to 5 per cent.

"The Scottish Widows' Fund, and many other offices, have of late years, by enlarging their sphere of investment, improved their average rate about $\frac{1}{2}$ per cent. bringing it to about $4\frac{1}{2}$ per cent. all round.

"But the larger the sums to be invested, and the greater the collective funds, the lower rules the rate of interest: for instance, at present (October 1867), many considerable mortgages and advances on *first class* debentures, are paying only 4 per cent."

Favourable inference. I should infer from this trustworthy information, that the Commissioners, having to invest considerable sums annually, would have no chance of getting $4\frac{1}{2}$ per cent., the rate got by the insurance companies; but might fairly expect to get more than $3\frac{1}{4}$ per cent., after paying all expenses. With compound interest at $3\frac{1}{2}$ per cent., a sum doubles in about 20 years, which is the period I have previously reckoned on : at that rate 1 £ would in 100 years become 32 £; and if we now set aside 25 millions £, and got 3½ per cent. upon it, our successors at the end of 100 years, would have 800 millions £, the present amount of our debt. We ought however, to set aside a larger sum, to allow for suspension during war.

The extensive field for investment now. It must be remembered that the field for investment is vastly greater now than it was a hundred years ago, fifty years ago, twenty years ago. Mr. R. L. Nash* estimates that in the short space of seven years, the public investments of the civilised world have amounted to a sum not much less than twice our national debt. When the entire investments are so fast increasing, secure investments for a few millions are found without much difficulty.

Objection: past experience. I am fully aware that many economists treat with contempt, any suggestion of the possibility of a government doing a thing which may be called trading, banking, or financing. They will say, government has tried lending : it has lent to Jamaica, to Greece, to Ireland during the famine : has it ever been repaid ? I reply that in those cases it made advances not because it had money to lend, but because considerations of policy required the rendering of assistance. The loans were made by Parliament on political grounds. If the sums set aside for a sinking-fund were to be dealt with in this way, I should despair of any advantage.

But the case different: loans for profit; The proceedings however, which I suggest, are quite different : I propose that money should be lent not for the

---

* Fenn on the Funds. 1867. xi.

benefit of the borrower, as in the case of Ireland when suffering from the extremities of famine, but for the benefit of the lender, just as happens with Insurance Companies, which certainly do not give up the principal they lend. I freely admit that the government would not realize the 4½ per cent. realized by the Scottish Widows' Fund ; the rate which the government would get would be less than this, because they would be rather more cautious in their choice of securities ; but this additional caution would make it the easier for them to secure the repayment of their principal.

made by a department of government. There is another important distinction. Loans like that made to Ireland, spring directly from Parliament : the loans I propose would be negociated by a *department* of government. The Commissioners would be responsible to Parliament, and their individual reputation and hopes of preferment would depend on the average rate they got : they would be called on to show why they got only 3¼ or 3¾ per cent., while the insurance companies were getting more by a fourth. Though the Cabinet cannot carry on money lending, the Commissioners might carry it on, and might be trusted to do it under the sharp criticism of the House of Commons. Nor is there any comparison here between the action of a government department and that of private firms : the comparison is between the action of a government *department* and that of the *managers* of a company ; between the action of one set of deputies and that of another set of deputies ; between the action of one set stimulated by annual *meetings* and the press, and the action of another set stimulated by annual *sessions* and the press.

Government departments not over generous. I do not find by experience that the actual government departments are lax in demanding the fulfilment of legal conditions. The Ordnance and the War Department require contractors to deliver the stipulated quantities of stores: the Custom House officers, and the Coast Guard, exert themselves to defeat the machinations of smugglers: the Excise officers have their eyes well open as to private stills: the Inland Revenue does its best to perform the impossible duty of exactly levying the income-tax. The Commissioners of the National Debt would, no doubt, exact the strict performance of agreements as to interest and repayment of loans. Even at present, as to the amounts lent to land-holders for drainage of their estates, I do not hear of any proposal to remit the principal, although these loans were made from considerations of policy, and not from any views of profit to government.

IV.

Apparent contradiction. THERE is, I know, an apparent contradiction here: I state that government might borrow at $3\frac{1}{4}$ per cent. and lend at $3\frac{1}{2}$ per cent. I maintain however, that this state of things is possible: it is similar to the case of bankers, who take money on deposit at 2 and lend it at 3 per cent. Will you then, turn the Commissioners into bankers and money-dealers? Not into bankers, but by all means into money-dealers, if the public may thus enjoy the benefit of a reduction of the National Debt. Besides, why should not the Commissioners be money-dealers, in the sense in which the managers of the Globe Insurance and the Scottish Widows' Fund are such?

Explained. It would of course be impossible for government to borrow at $3\frac{1}{4}$ per cent., and then, on the same conditions, to lend at more than $3\frac{1}{4}$. But the conditions are not the same.

Consols: why low interest. First, as to Consols : their conditions are very singular, and their popularity is very great. I have already* quoted Mr. Newmarch's article on Mr. Pitt's Loans ;† an article far too little known :‡ it is there explained why it is that government can borrow most advantageously in 3 per cent. stocks, and why it is that virtually, they cannot borrow at all at par.

---

* Chap. II. Sect. 13.
† *Statistical Journal.* 18. 130.
‡ I say that this article is too little known, because able men continue to censure Mr. Pitt for not having borrowed in stocks at higher interest. It is said that the right practice would be to borrow at par, and to leave the lenders to fix the rate current at the date of the loan. (*Dict. de l'Écon. Pol.* I. 684. 1.) Such theoretical financiers would be convinced of their ignorance if they would read Mr. Newmarch. They have forgotten that government always borrows on this singular condition: that though the lender can never demand the repayment of his principal, government is at liberty to repay it at any time (with a year's notice indeed in the case of Consols). The lenders object to a 4, 5, or 6 per cent. stock, because they know that in a few years it will be reduced to a $3\frac{1}{2}$ or 3 per cent. stock. To protect themselves, they either refuse to lend at all in high-rated stocks, or demand such an extravagant rate as to make the loan impossible. Government has no choice therefore; it must borrow in a low-rated stock: unless indeed, it will abandon the conditions of repayment, in which case there would be no advantage in borrowing at high interest.

To illustrate the principle: suppose that with Consols at 50, government offered to borrow at par, and I had 10,000£ at command. If I buy old Consols on the Stock Exchange, I shall get 6 per cent. in perpetuity. If government insists on borrowing at par, and if I take 6 per cent., I shall for the present get the same 6 per cent. interest as if I bought Consols at 50: but I shall not get it in perpetuity; for whenever government can borrow at a less rate than 6 per cent. it will pay me off, or will compel me to take a lower rate: thus my 6 per cent. will gradually fall to 5, 4, or 3 per cent. I therefore refuse to lend to government at par; or I demand such extravagant compensation as the government will not give.

Add the consideration, that in buying Consols at 50, I have a reasonable expectation of finding my principal gradually increase from 10,000£ up to 15,000, or perhaps 20,000£; whereas if I lend the 10,000£ at 6 per cent., the principal cannot increase.

The government therefore, cannot borrow at par or in high-rated stocks, so long as old 3 per cent. stocks are to be bought.

Mr. Newmarch's explanation. We have already seen that in the great market of the Stock Exchange, certain conditions have actually come into existence : that stocks fulfilling those conditions are peculiarly current; and that Consols bear the highest price because they fulfil those conditions in the highest degree. Stocks must be marketable : they must be understood by all : they must have no new conditions attached to them : they must be free from uncertain contingencies. Consols fulfil all these conditions; with this additional advantage, that they cannot be redeemed without a year's notice.

The action of the Court of Chancery and of Trustees. A second cause of increased value to Consols and to other 3 per cents., is the preference given to them by the Court of Chancery for the investment of trust funds; and this not only for trusts managed by the Court, but for the vast number of private trusts subject to the Court's jurisdiction. Of late years no doubt, many trustees have received powers to invest in other securities, such as preferential railway stocks and debentures; but where the amounts are large, where the income is deemed of less importance than the preservation of the principal, and where the trustees are more intent on their own ease than on the interests of the present beneficiaries, the 3 per cent. funds still have the preference.

Therefore Government can borrow on 3 per cent. stocks at lowest market rate, The 3 per cent. stocks being thus in greater demand than other securities bearing the same interest, and being regarded as of higher value by bodies having in the aggregate very large investments to make, it follows that their price will be relatively higher than that of other securities : which is the same thing as saying, that investors will lend upon 3 per cent. stocks at a lower rate than upon other stocks.

and generally at singularly low interest. But even on other and less marketable stocks, government can borrow under the market rate: for the obvious reason that its credit stands higher than that of any individual or any corporation; and this not only because for nearly 200 years it has never failed in an engagement, but also because the nation is free from the danger of revolution at home and of conquest by foreigners. Holland is eminent for good faith and for inexhaustible resources; it far surpasses us in efforts to reduce the debt; but it is a small country, exposed to be again overrun by its neighbour: its government therefore, has nothing like the credit of ours, and cannot borrow at nearly so low a rate.*

Part of Explanation. We begin to see then, an explanation of the apparent contradiction, in the statement that the Commissioners of the national debt might lend their funds at a rate above that at which the Chancellor of the Exchequer could borrow: that is, that the government could borrow with one hand at $3\frac{1}{4}$ per cent., and at the same time lend with the other at $3\frac{1}{2}$ or 4 per cent. The government can borrow in any stock below the market rate, because its credit is of the very highest, because its good faith is unquestionable and its resources are unbounded: it can borrow still further under the market rate in 3 per cent. stocks, because these are peculiarly marketable, and because large amounts are taken up by the Court of Chancery, and by Trustees under the Court's jurisdiction.

Could Commissioners get market rate? The only question now is whether the Commissioners could lend their funds at the market rate; that is at a rate exceeding $3\frac{1}{4}$ per cent. I will not pronounce absolutely that

---

* Block, " Puissance Comparée," pa. 166.

they could; but I see no reason why they should not. I have pointed out that trustees of private property get 4½ per cent. without infringing any legal rule : I concede however, that they lend in such sums as 2,000£ or 3,000£, which perhaps are smaller than Commissioners could deal with. I have shown that the Scottish Widows' Fund, dealing with millions of money, earned formerly 4 per cent., and of late years 4½ per cent. : I know no reason why the Commissioners should not earn more than 3¼.

Loans for long periods: modern extension of financial operations. The Commissioners could lend for long fixed periods ; for 20, 50, or 100 years : borrowers for such periods are obliged to pay a high rate. Municipal corporations borrow habitually for 30 years, with a provision for an annual repayment of part of the principal : they have to pay 4, 4½, or 5 per cent., even where the security of the rates is ample. The railroad companies often have to pay 5 per cent. even on debentures. Bad as is the credit of railways at present, the losses of debenture holders are trifling; and if Commissioners had invested in them, they would have gained a high rate of interest, after deducting any losses they might have sustained. I say nothing of guaranteed Indian securities, because I should doubt the propriety of going outside the three kingdoms, and this not so much from financial as from political considerations. Such investments as I am speaking of are far easier to find now than they were formerly : the railroads with hundreds of millions of capital, have accustomed the public to deal with vast sums of money.

I think they could so lend. I make no pretension to pronounce dogmatically what rate Commissioners could get : but I cannot doubt that they could get more than 3¼ per cent., which is about the rate at which the government can borrow in ordinary times : nor can I doubt that they could get so much more than 3¼ per cent. as to pay the expenses of the Commission and leave a surplus.

Conclusion of explanation. This then explains the contradiction of which I am apparently guilty, when I assume that one department of government might borrow at 3¼ per cent., while another department was lending at 3½, 3¾, or 4 per cent. The explanation is that the Chancellor of the Exchequer would borrow at 3 per cent. in a stock highly marketable, in great demand for trust investments, and supported by the reputation of a nation unfailing in its engagements, protected by its geographical position, and possessed of unfailing resources : while the Commissioners would lend to corporate bodies, companies, or landholders, for long fixed periods, with a little risk of occasional loss. We know by experience that the Chancellor can borrow at 3¼ per cent. : we know also by experience that borrowers for long fixed periods are obliged to pay 4 to 4½ per cent. If the Commissioners could be entrusted with discretionary powers, subject to the requirement of an annual report to Parliament, I do not see why they should not gain a rate of interest, approaching the 4 to 4½ per cent. gained by the directors of the Scottish Widows' Fund. A sinking-fund so managed would accumulate fast.

V.

Even if no profit, yet Public Opinion. BUT even if the arrangement yielded no profit, if the Commissioners after paying their expenses and recouping occasional losses, only earned the rate of interest at which the Chancellor of the Exchequer borrowed, I should still maintain the advantage of the system: I should still hold it desirable that sums set apart for a sinking-fund should be placed in the hands of Commissioners, and that they should invest those sums in securities other than government stocks. The greatest advantage I see in this arrangement is not the profit; this I regard as secondary: the greatest advantage is the making the sinking-fund intelligible to all: I believe that there would be hope of permanence, if Parliament and the country received an annual account, to the effect that the sinking-fund, which was last year 57 millions £ is this year 61 millions £, and that the whole of this 61 millions £ is invested in loans and debentures and not in government stocks. We should all understand a statement: owing 801 millions £; assets 61 millions £: balance of liabilities 740 millions £. Such a state of accounts would put our finances under the guarantee of public opinion. But if we were told, as formerly, that the debt was 801 millions £, of which 61 millions £ was redeemed, we should most of us be doubtful as to the real meaning, and should not be ready to check any Chancellor of the Exchequer who was disposed to tamper with the fund; and under this latter mode of investment and of account, the guarantee of public opinion would cease.

VI.

What amount? As Holland? I HAVE assumed that the nation is unwilling to make any great effort, such as would be required to rival the proceedings of Holland, where the amount of debt annually paid off is, population for population, equal to 15 millions £ a year for us. Doubtless we might do this: during a short part of the Crimean war we paid 1s. 4d. in the £ as income-tax; and that same rate now levied would bring us up to about the level of Holland. This is not to be thought of: nor is it with reference to such efforts that I have recommended the practice of investing in general securities. I may even concede, that Holland, exposed to the ambitious attacks of her powerful neighbours, has peculiarly strong reasons for husbanding her resources, and for lessening the charges that weigh on her government.

Circumstances on which I found my argument. The circumstances too, on which I have founded my argument; the fluctuations generally occurring in human affairs; the probability that modern English prosperity will be followed by a less prosperous condition; the more than possibility that our manufacturing and commercial preponderance will be reduced; the obvious diminution in our reserve of coal; these circumstances, while they furnish strong grounds for urging the diminution of the debt, do not peremptorily call on us for overwhelming present sacrifice. I feel that it is vain to dwell on the manifest truth, which we have learnt to disregard, that each generation at present pays the debt once in the form of interest, and still leaves the 800 millions of principal as a legacy to its sons : and vain to urge the manifest inference, make a supreme effort and discharge the debt. I must be content to found my remonstrance on those minor circumstances which may be summed up in the maxim, during prosperity make ready for adversity.

Suppose principal of thirty What amount then, must we raise in order to extinguish our present debt in *millions: how long would take?* 100 years? Let us suppose that we shortly accumulated in the hands of the Commissioners, as much as 30 millions £. This sum doubled five times would amount to 960 millions £, an ample sum for our purpose. Since the Commissioners would always reinvest their income, and thus earn compound interest, if they could get 5 per cent., they would double their principal about every 14 years; and in little more than 71 years they would raise their 30 millions to 960 millions. At 4 per cent. each period instead of 14 years would be about 18 years; and to bring 30 millions up to 960 millions would require about 89 years: at $3\frac{1}{2}$ per cent. each period would be a little over 20 years; and 101 years would be necessary to rise to 960 millions.*

We surely could raise thirty millions £. If then we could once get a fund of 30 millions £, we might hope to extinguish the debt in 100 years, or less. Surely, to raise 30 millions is no hopeless task. One year of war would oblige us to raise it and that in a single year: cannot we do as much for a purpose of peace and security, and that too, spreading the effort over several years? It would be undesirable to raise it at once: it would probably be better the first year to begin with a million, in order that the Commissioners might feel their way as to investments: afterwards let the annual sum be increased, and the 30 millions be completed if possible, in 7 or 10 years. Let all of it be got by an income-tax, so that no dis-

---

* The time necessary for doubling a sum of money at compound interest, is at 5 per cent $14\frac{1}{4}$ years, at 4 per cent. $17\frac{3}{4}$ years, at $3\frac{1}{2}$ per cent. 20 years, at 3 per cent. $23\frac{1}{4}$ years, at $2\frac{1}{2}$ per cent. 28 years. But this is on the assumption that the interest is paid once a year: in practice it is paid twice a year: at 5 per cent. therefore, the period required is only 14 years instead of $14\frac{1}{4}$; half of the period required at $2\frac{1}{2}$ per cent. with interest paid once a year.

turbance might be caused in our fiscal arrangements, and no hindrance be offered to remission of taxation. Would any taxpayers be found so unpatriotic as to object to pay "the sinking-fund penny," or "the sinking-fund threepence," being once convinced that 7 or 10 years would end the demand, and that extinction of the present debt would follow?

VII.

Future Loans. FURTHER loans no doubt, will be contracted. Since 1815 however, we have avoided any increase on the whole, and we have even diminished the debt a little. We have borrowed 20 millions for slave compensation; 9 millions to relieve Irish distress; 37 millions for Crimean war expenses; 5 millions for fortifications: but by the creation of terminable annuities, and by the application of surplus income, we have paid off these debts. We need not make any special provision in this respect, though I think that besides the establishment of a sinking-fund, we should do wisely to actually pay off a little faster in time of peace, in order to get a provision in readiness. We ought to keep the amount down to 800 millions as a maximum: to do this we should reduce it during peace to 750 or 700 millions; and we could then occasionally borrow 50 or 100 millions without exceeding the total of 800 millions.

May be paid off by other means. The measure I have already mentioned, as proposed by Mr. Gladstone, and candidly adopted by Mr. Disraeli, by which the savings' bank funds are turned into terminable annuities, will in fact considerably reduce the present debt. The

Life Annuities which are sold, and the systematic quarterly application of one-fourth of any annual surplus, give help in the same direction. These means may be sufficient to keep the debt down to its present 800 millions.

War would require loans. Undoubtedly we may again be drawn into long and expensive wars. Should such misfortunes occur, it is certain that we shall again be great borrowers; for even the Crimean war, although of moderate dimensions, and although we fed it with an income-tax of 1s. 2d. and 1s. 4d. in the £, outran our powers of taxation, and added millions to our debt.

Cost of war now, War too, while it lasts, is more costly than ever: the number of soldiers employed being vast, and the cost of arms and ammunition enormous. On the other hand, even those who believe in the probability of wars, must concede that they are likely to be short. Formerly, the United Provinces were in a state of hostility with Spain during a century: the notorious Thirty Years' War ruined a generation of Germans, and permanently impoverished their country: the French Revolution and Napoleon kept Europe in hostilities during twenty years.

On the other hand, the experience of Austria proves to us how rapidly a contest may be ended: Solferino and Magenta first, and Sadowa afterwards, have shown at what a pace military affairs now proceed. Battles formerly indeed, were as decisive as they are now: but months were necessary to bring the hostile armies together; a year slipped away in transportation of troops: now, through steamers and railroads distance has ceased to operate. War therefore, though expensive while it lasts, will probably cost less than formerly, because it will be short.

and of armed peace. It is not war, but chronic preparation for war, which is now oppressive. It has lately been calculated* that the European powers are spending nearly 80 millions £ a year on their peace establishments, and are employing 2 million men at least. Armed peace may be more costly than war.

Favourable to avoidance of debt. However this may be, the present condition of affairs is favourable to our avoidance of debt. Our expenses are annual and are annually provided for. We are spending something like 25 millions a year on our army and navy; that is 500 millions every 20 years. If, according to our former fashion, and according to the present American fashion, we reduced our yearly expense to 5 millions, when war broke out we should have everything to do in a hurry; our budget would require a sudden and great increase in taxation, and we should be driven to borrow largely.

Conclusion. I am neither defending nor attacking our present practice; I only say that it tends to the payment for our forces by annual taxation: whereas our old practice of deferring preparations till war broke out, tended to the payment very much by loans. We may hope therefore, that our heavy actual taxation, together with our sincere present hatred of war, will, in the absence of another revolution of '89, save us from large future loans; and that what debt we do incur may be discharged, as debt incurred since 1815 has been discharged, by selling life annuities, by applying our occasional surplus income, and by other informal arrangements. If this should prove to be the case, then such a sinking-fund as I am recommending, would in less than a hundred years see us freed from all debt, as Prussia and Sweden are now:

---

* *Economist*, 1254. 1015. 2.

and as we may hope, with this honourable addition, that we had never failed in our national engagements.

VIII.

War under sinking-fund of 1786. IT will be remembered that in 1786, Mr. Fox moved a resolution, willingly accepted by Mr. Pitt, that the Commissioners of the national debt should be at liberty to lend their funds to government when a loan was to be made. I have pointed out that in a few years war broke out and loans were contracted; and that this was the cause of the failure of the sinking-fund. I do not mean by this that Mr. Fox's resolution was the cause of that failure: I am convinced that under any circumstances the same course would have been pursued; that the million of taxes handed to the Commissioners would certainly have found its way back to the Exchequer, whenever the resources of the country were hard pressed. It would have been better during continued war, to suspend the payment of the million to the Commissioners.

In future, the Commissioners must sometimes lend to government, Ought the Commissioners in future to lend their funds to the Exchequer? Let us hope that peace might continue long enough to enable us to accumulate the proposed 30 millions £: the Commissioners would have to invest annually the interest on this sum, and on all future accumulations; that is, their annual investment would begin at a million, and would increase to a much larger sum. I have stated my preference for investments other than government stocks, on the grounds of a higher rate of interest, and still more of the greater simplicity of accounts, and the consequent possibility of putting the fund under the guarantee of public opinion. But it is vain to hope that in times of national difficulty, the Commissioners could refuse to lend their annual income to the Exchequer. Nor would the perplexity be great, if the Commissioners in their annual account, exhibited their assets as consisting principally of mortgages and debentures, and to a small extent of Consols: this would be very different from the old form:—debt 700 millions £, of which 200 millions £ redeemed.

viz., when Consols are low. The general rule would probably be that the Commissioners should buy government stocks, or take part of a new loan, whenever by doing so they could obtain a higher rate of interest than by investing otherwise. If Consols fell to 70, they would get more than 4 per cent., in perpetuity, besides the hope of the 70 rising to 90 in a few years: at such a price, Consols might prove to be far their best investment.

IX.

CONCLUSIONS.

IN this last chapter I propound a scheme which seems to me practicable. I remark again that Mr. Pitt's plan broke down because it went too far, in trying to carry on the process of extinction during war; and also because it was unintelligible to the nation, and therefore failed to secure the guarantee of public opinion. I object to the conversion of the stocks into terminable annuities, on this ground of its rendering the scheme unintelligible, as well as on the admitted ground of wastefulness.

The scheme I propose is merely a modification of that of 1786 : it is not one of raising an annual surplus and applying it directly to extinction, because we should probably lose in this way the advantage of compound interest.

What I suggest is that a principal sum shall be raised, by instalments, in a few years, and shall be placed in the hands of Commissioners, who shall invest it, not in government stocks, but in such securities as are held by the great Insurance Companies. The public would easily understand the annual accounts :—"the nation owes 800 millions £; it holds securities worth 50 millions £ which are accumulating at compound interest."

I state my belief that the Commissioners might realize a higher rate than the $3\frac{1}{4}$ per cent. obtainable by Consols; for I show that one great Insurance Company, on smaller amounts indeed, formerly got 4, and now gets $4\frac{1}{2}$ per cent. I notice the apparent contradiction in saying that government could borrow at $3\frac{1}{4}$ per cent., and could at the same time lend at $3\frac{1}{2}$ or 4 : I explain it by the fact that government borrows in Consols which have a peculiar and artificial value, and on which the interest therefore, is unusually low; whereas the sinking-fund Commissioners would lend for long fixed periods, on securities not marketable on the Stock Exchange; conditions that are found in fact to cause a comparatively high rate of interest. I conclude that even if the Commissioners could get, after paying expenses, only the same $3\frac{1}{4}$ per cent. which they could get from Consols, this private investment would be preferable because more generally intelligible.

As to the amount of the fund, I mention 30

million £ as the sum which, if accumulated at compound interest, would probably pay off our present debt in about 100 years: the 30 million £ to be raised gradually, and at first slowly, to enable the Commissioners to invest it to the greatest advantage. This moderate sum being once raised, no further surplus taxation would be needed: the only future operation would be the annual investment of the accruing interest, and the reinvestment of securities at maturity.

Future debt would have to be dealt with as it arose, either by a separate sinking-fund or by additions to this one. Any great and continued war would no doubt cause great increase of debt: but the tendency of war at present is to be short and decisive; vastly expensive for a year or two, and above all requiring a perpetual armed peace, a state of things which in England causes rather a constant drain on regular taxation than the accumulation of great war debts.

Finally, remembering Mr. Fox's clause in 1786, I ask whether in case of war loans, the Commissioners would be required to take a part of such loans so far as any moneys were at their command. I reply that if that investment were the most profitable which offered, they should certainly be required to take it: I even go further, and say that under the pressure of public necessity they should be required to waive the question of profit altogether, though at the risk of extending beyond the stipulated hundred years the final extinction of our present debt.

THE END.

BIRMINGHAM:
PRINTED BY MARTIN BILLING, SON, AND CO., LIVERY STREET.

www.ingramcontent.com/pod-product-compliance
Lightning Source LLC
Chambersburg PA
CBHW021358230426
43666CB00006B/562